THE FIREMAN'S
Wife

THE FIREMAN'S
Wife

Susan Farren

HYPERION NEW YORK

Library of Congress Cataloging-in-Publication Data

Farren, Susan
    The fireman's wife / by Susan Farren.—1st ed.
        p.   cm.
    ISBN 1-4013-0173-8
    1. Farren, Susan—Relations with men.   2. Farren, Dan—Family.
3. Fire fighters—Family relationships.   4. Fire fighters' spouses—
United States—Biography.   5. Fire fighters—United States—
Biography.   6. Wives—United States—Family relationships.
7. Fire extinction—Accidents—California—Petaluma.   I. Title.

    TH9118.F37A3   2005
    363.37'092—dc22
    [B]
                                                    2005040404

Hyperion books are available for special promotions and premiums. For details contact Michael Rentas, Assistant Director, Inventory Operations, Hyperion, 77 West 66th Street, 11th floor, New York, New York 10023, or call 212-456-0133.

FIRST EDITION

10   9   8   7   6   5   4   3   2   1

This book is dedicated to my husband, Dan, whose faith and commitment to our family and his career made this story possible, and to our tribe of miniature firefighters, Ben, Donna-Bailey, Matthew, Roman, and Michael. You are my light and my joy.

In loving memory of my mentor and friend Flight Nurse Erin Eachus Reed March 23, 1957–September 29, 2005

THE FIREMAN'S
Wife

PROLOGUE

THE FIREMAN'S HEART POUNDED, his thickly gloved hand gripping the ladder's beam. The whispered words of men who'd been here before him jogged through his mind: "Breathe slowly, think about what you're doing, don't waste the air pack." He began his determined ascent, one heavy boot after another.

The fire had begun in a recently vacated barbershop in a row of landmark buildings. The source of ignition was a box of personal belongings stored too closely to a water heater. A call to 911 reported smoke and flames, and the first fire engines arrived within moments. Identifying the immediate danger to the adjacent buildings in this historic area of Petaluma, the first officer on scene called for mutual aid. Engines responded from local stations and neighboring towns; off-duty personnel were called in as reinforcements. Firefighters began strategically surrounding the picturesque row of shops and businesses, attacking the rapidly spreading fire from positions on the ground, rooftops, and aerial ladders.

The fireman eased himself onto the roof of a threatened building nearby. With a chain saw and axe, he prepared to "trench-cut" the roof and interrupt the fire's path of destruction. Crouching on one knee, he assessed the situation through the smoke's haze, acknowledged his captain, and brought the saw to life.

Amid the low rumble of fire and the deafening roar of water from a ladder truck seventy feet away, the radio clipped to his chest went unheard.

Atop the ladder perched high above the flames, the officer directing the water's flow struggled to see through the dense smoke. Readjusting the nozzle, he was momentarily blinded. A moment was all it took: a stream of water exiting at fifteen hundred gallons a minute hit the fireman trench-cutting the roof below.

The water struck with the force of a cannon. The chain saw flew from the fireman's gloved hands. He struggled to regain his footing, twisting and turning against the force pushing him closer to the roof's edge. Ten, twenty, thirty feet tumbled by as he grasped for something to hold on to. Battling for leverage, his body was slammed backward into a parapet wall, his air pack catching on the edge just inches from the fully engulfed building below. Pain seared through his back and chest. He gasped for breath, his lungs burning from the lack of oxygen. "Dear God, don't let me die."

Firemen began appearing out of nowhere, setting into motion a frenzy of activity. The Rapid Intervention Crew, an expertly trained group of paramedics and firefighters, were deployed to the roof. The fireman's air pack was quickly removed and sent sliding down the steeply pitched roof. An oxygen mask and cervical collar were positioned as he was strapped into a basket. His body, lowered off the building by the very truck whose master stream had struck him only moments before, was set into the hands of await-ing firefighters. "I . . . can't . . . breathe . . ." he gasped as they prepared to load him into an ambulance. Locking eyes with a fellow firefighter, he struggled to speak.

"Call . . . my . . . wife."

I AM

I AM THANKFUL. This has not always been an easy walk for me.

I am disappointed. We have missed family gatherings, weddings, dinner engagements, birthday parties, and holidays because of shift schedules and overtime.

I am patient. There have been dinners spent at the firehouse waiting for Daddy to return from a call while the kids get cranky and the food gets cold.

I am nervous. I awake at 3:00 A.M. hearing creaks in the house and don't have the comfort of my husband beside me.

I am tired. The house is full of sick kids and there is no relief in sight because Daddy is on a seventy-two-hour shift.

I am jealous. Jealous of all the women whose husbands came home at 5:00 P.M. to have dinner and hold them at the end of their day.

I am worried. I worry that he may not come home one day. This I try to tuck away.

I am content. We have decided to give up my career so I can stay home and raise our children. We no longer have an abundance of money or things. It is the greatest freedom I have ever known.

I am incompetent. There was a time when I considered myself moderately intelligent. I now struggle to remember where I left my car keys, the diaper bag, and, occasionally, the baby.

I am waiting. Knowing the phone may one day ring for me.

I am doubting. Doubting that God hears all my prayers.

Doubting I am the kind of wife and mother He needs me to be.

I am trusting. Trusting that my husband will come home again.

I am confident, I am embarrassed, I am lonely, I am surprised, I am overworked, I am underpaid.

I am . . . The Fireman's Wife.

SQUAD 51

~~

MY HUSBAND, DAN, has always wanted to be a fireman. He was introduced to his destiny as a boy, by two men who visited his home every week to share their escapades as firefighter/paramedics. Their stories transported him to the very homes where life-and-death decisions were made, exposing him to the victories, frustrations, and struggles these men faced every day. He was captivated by them, awestruck by their bravery, knowledge, and quick decision making. He was determined to be just like them.

His mother tells stories of her perpetually cheerful, tow-headed boy whirling around the neighborhood on his Big Wheel, lunch box turned first aid kit held tightly in his lap. He would race to the scraped knees and wounded pride of any number of kids who injured themselves in their quiet, middle-income, suburban neighborhood. Injured kids would sooner run to the door of Danny's modest two-story home for help than to their own mothers. "Go get Danny" came to their minds long before they'd learned the phrase "Go call 911."

Small and athletic, this gregarious middle child, flanked on either end by sisters, found the outlet for his natural agility and boy-driven interests not in sports, like many of his friends, but in everything related to firemen and rescuers. Fireman costumes and rescuing neighbor kids would, over the years, evolve into working at a first aid station at the local theme park, attending firefighting and Emergency Medical Technician (EMT) courses at the local junior college, and finally enrolling in paramedic school.

But during his childhood years, stories from the two men who he later referred to as his mentors would have to suffice. The commitment he saw displayed every week in the faces of those firefighters was enough to plant the seeds for his future.

Those two men were Johnny Gage and Roy DeSoto from the popular TV show *Emergency*. Their TV characters instilled commitment and inspiration into the heart of the boy who would one day become my husband, desires that were solidified by the view inside an ambulance.

On an unseasonably warm day in September of his fifth-grade year, Dan and a friend decided to have some late-afternoon fun riding around the neighborhood. The bicycle alone not providing enough entertainment for the two of them, they gravitated to something more interesting: turning Dan's bike into a towing device. A rope was tied to the back, allowing a passenger to ride behind the bike on a skateboard. Dan's mother, seeing the little inventors, had come out at one point and asked them to remove the rope, arguing that it presented too much potential for an accident. The boys acknowledged their understanding: the understanding that they needed to take their antics further down the street. The towing device was a hit, drawing a number of kids eager to participate with their go-carts and skateboards, Dan judicially ensuring that each kid had a chance for a ride.

A shout for dinner brought the festivities to an end and sent Dan blazing back home with the tow rope bouncing merrily behind him. A quick loop around the front of his mother's car, parallel-parked on the street in front of their home, and he would glide into the vacant driveway for a perfect landing. But the rope cut unexpectedly short under the car's front fender, the knot catching under the tire. Catapulted like a rider from a mechanical bull, Dan was launched over the handlebars headfirst onto the edge of a curb. He lay unconscious for several moments before a neighbor, screaming for help, ran the limp, pint-sized body up the driveway. Dan woke in the back of an ambulance, its siren screaming a path to the local hospital. Looking up at the rescuers, he thought quite simply, "If I live through this, I'll be doing this when I grow up for the rest of my life."

After five days in the hospital and with a new appreciation for his mother's advice, the little fireman was released to recover from his skull fracture with a career path set firmly in his mind.

But as any firefighter can attest, this career is not a matter of choice alone. Time, training, and experience would be necessary before the future fireman would be eligible to apply for a job. When that time finally came eight years later, when Dan was eighteen, departmental quotas for diversity—designed to make departments more reflective of the communities they served—left a young man with Irish heritage at the bottom of the hiring list. He was neither the right gender nor ancestry to fit the bill. It was a very different rejection than his ancestors faced so many years ago when the great potato famine sent thousands of Irish and Scottish immigrants flooding to the East Coast of the United States. Factories and storefronts placed signs in their windows: "NINA"—No Irish Need Apply. White-collar discrimination led the Irish to the jobs no one else wanted, jobs that were dirty or dangerous or both—firefighters and police officers. Dan now craved the job his great-great-grandfathers had been forced to do. But interview after interview left him without the job he longed for.

The arduous process of filling out applications, taking physical agility tests, reviewing interview questions, and visiting firehouses in an effort to learn more about each department would be in vain. His chances of providing emergency care appeared to be better on the streets with his Big Wheel than inside the fire service.

Two years went by without a job offer from a fire department, a time he cheerfully refers to as his "interview perfection training." It gave him a compassion for the eagerness and frustration he would see in the faces of other would-be firefighters. But that time was not wasted. He landed a job at a private ambulance service and began to hone his skills as a paramedic, eventually being promoted to the position of paramedic supervisor. It was during these important times that he began training, or "precepting," other paramedics.

He loved being able to pass on his experience and training to other young men and women who found themselves drawn to this line of work. He discovered a terrific network of friends and found a common bond with the public safety folks he worked with on a daily basis. Firefighters, police officers, nurses, and doctors all seemed to have the same intrinsic desire to help people and make right what too often seemed to go so wrong. But the privately owned ambulance companies didn't afford the one thing so many paramedics needed: job security. Although a private ambulance paramedic could make a decent living, it was without the benefits and support found in the career of firefighting. Most importantly, there was no fighting fires, which Dan longed for, so he continued the process of applying and testing at fire departments.

Dan had been invited to a paramedic partner's house for dinner by a mutual friend of ours, a party I had also been invited to. Introductions were made, and the evening progressed with small talk eventually turning to street stories, a theme that's played out anytime firefighters, police officers, or paramedics get together for social functions. I admired the way Dan spoke about his patients with respect and concern, and watched the way his dark, compassionate eyes reflected the intensity of his feelings one moment and then danced as he fell into laughter the next. He was refreshingly kind and humble, while still possessing an air of confidence. There was something magnetic about this man, not that I was interested, as I had sworn off men in the business of emergency care. Recently transitioning out of working as a paramedic myself, I was tired of the dating scene and was hoping to settle down with someone with a more predictable line of work than public safety. Dan had been clear: although he loved emergency care, his real desire was to be a fireman. It didn't matter how interesting he appeared, that was a line of work I was not interested in being a part of. Dan was nice, but clearly not the man for me.

Six weeks later, at a dinner party, I saw him again, shockingly aware that I stood frozen across the room staring at the man I was going to marry. I had yet to hold his hand or spend a moment alone with him, but I knew. That moment brought truth to the words my mother had so often spoken to me, and as my grandmother had after my mother's passing, that when I met the man who was meant for me I would just know. At twenty-eight years old I figured I had somehow missed the "just knowing" part and had resorted to the "just hunting" method. My established criteria—tall, dark, and handsome, with a normal job— had just been tossed out the window for short, bald, and funny who wants to be a fireman. Eighteen months later we walked down the aisle as husband and wife, our unpredictable future ahead of us.

THE STING OF REJECTION

~⌒~

With the newness of married life and its subsequent adjustments and transitions, my husband spoke little of his desire to be a firefighter. I'm sure I had mentioned on several occasions that I would be delighted if he did something other than firefighting, so the topic was not regularly addressed. This did not mean that his intentions had changed; it only meant that he wasn't discussing them with me.

Within a year his dark-blue suit was out of its protective cover and he was once again shining his shoes in preparation for the interviews that were sure to follow the applications he had been turning in. I eventually found myself sitting across the dining room table peppering him with mock interview questions to help him prepare for the job I didn't want him to have. I received an education in the process, as I became aware of how stressful and challenging the course of employment could be. Helping to prepare him for the job was preparing me to understand what he would be going through if he did get hired somewhere. It gave me a whole new respect for a career I had thought was defined by driving a fire truck and, as they say at the firehouse, "squirting the wet stuff on the red stuff."

Never did I realize the knowledge base these men and women would need in order to anticipate the life-threatening changes that can take place in a fire. Wind direction, fire temperature, fuel sources, water pressure, and hose sizes are all things that must be considered in any given moment when attacking even what seems like a simple blaze. One wrong decision and someone could be hurt or, worse, lose their life. It was mind-boggling to me, as we spent hours reviewing the history of the fire service and the advances in technology that affect what is still one of man's greatest enemies. With fire being capable of indiscriminately destroying lives, homes, and land, it is treated with the greatest respect by those who fight it. Their respect for what they refer to as "The Beast," "The Dragon," or "The Red Devil" binds them together like a tribe of warriors. The fact that they refer to firefighting as a "brotherhood" would be a clear indication of the intimacy and loyalty reserved for those who choose to enter into the life of a fire-fighter.

The history of the fire service reads like a perpetual world war. Mankind has learned to both fear and befriend this miraculous thing, which can either help or harm us. We use fire to prepare our food, warm our bodies, and in some cases ward off our enemies. The conditional part of the relationship requires respect and boundaries, as without containment this friend becomes an opportunistic monster with an insatiable appetite. Given the right conditions, it will devour everything in its path, growing stronger and more ravenous with each passing moment.

Poring over the annals of firefighting, I learned about the pride and honor that are passed along like heirlooms in firefighting families. Many of the men and women who find themselves in this profession aren't there by chance, but by bloodline. Although many of us have lost sight of our family traditions and heritages, there is a bounty of firefighters who can proudly count out more than two or three forefathers who were "on the job." Dan's own great-grandfather, his namesake, helped fight the fires from the 1906 earthquake in San Francisco. The legacy skipped two generations and landed squarely in the heart of my husband.

This history lesson brought with it a treasure chest of information about the little-known symbols of the legacy that are still maintained today. The international firefighting symbol, known as the Maltese Cross, is still seen on uniforms, vehicle stickers, and logos the world over. It is the firefighter's insignia of protection, considered a badge of honor, and comes with a story of its own.

Hundreds of years ago a band of Crusaders from the island of Malta, known as the Knights of St. John, were fighting in the Crusades for the Holy Land. Their enemies, the Saracens, attacked them with an unexpected weapon: glass bombs filled with a flammable oil called naphtha, followed by flaming torches or arrows. Hundreds of Knights were burned alive; others risked their own lives to save their brothers-in-arms from dying such a painful death. The life-savers' heroic efforts were recognized by fellow Crusaders, who awarded each hero a badge of honor marked by a cross, similar to the one firefighters wear today. The symbol is a reminder that the one who wears it is willing to lay down his or her life for their fellow man, as the Knights of St. John did so many years ago.

My husband's heritage brought its own contribution to the fire service. When Irish firefighters were killed in the line of duty, their family funerals were filled with the traditions of the homeland, meaning bagpipes were played. Those who attended the funerals were exposed to the mournful and haunting sounds of the pipes, which brought an air of dignity to the solemn occasion. The power of the pipes somehow made it okay for the hardened firefighters to let their guard down and weep for their fallen comrades. Pipe bands from the East Coast representing both fire and police now have more than sixty uniformed pipers each, many who will dress in the traditional kilt and tunic of the Scottish or Irish. Today the pipes have become expected at the funerals of fallen heroes throughout the world.

My heart was overcome with pride and gratefulness as I read about the efforts and sacrifices made for centuries that bring us to the honorable, albeit imperfect, world of firefighting as we know it today.

The fire service has come a long way. Just 250 years ago, fire brigades were passing buckets of water in an effort to put out blazes. These rudimentary groups were eventually replaced in pre-Revolutionary times by hand tubs, enormous iron-tired tubs weighing up to three tons. The firemen who dragged them to the scene were often so exhausted from the effort that they would have to call on bystanders to do the pumping.

In time, horses were trained to drag the behemoth devices. Horses eventually gave way to steam engines, and then the rapid improvements of the automobile. Today's fire engines are luxurious by comparison to their predecessors. Fully enclosed, leather-seated, air-conditioned units with radios and computers are common, and worth every penny of the half million dollars invested in them.

Vast improvements in equipment, uniforms, helmets,

and breathing apparatuses as well as incredible advances in the techniques of firefighting dramatically reduce some of the dangers that firefighters faced as little as fifty years ago. While these rapid advances did little to soothe the trepidation I felt about my husband's career goals, I started to feel proud of his desire to be part of something so courageous.

It isn't just the equipment that has evolved over the years. The classic statement that the fire service is "two hundred years of tradition unimpeded by progress" couldn't be further from the truth. Like any long-standing profession, change takes place reluctantly, but change takes place nonetheless.

Example: for as long as firefighters have been putting out fires, ambulance companies have been caring for the sick and injured. Many times their jobs intertwine, as a car accident creates a situation where a patient has to be extricated from the vehicle (done by the fire department), and then the patient's care is transferred to the folks on the ambulance.

The first calls for help would send both professions rushing to the scene. In many instances fire engine personnel would arrive a few moments before the ambulance. This inevitably put the firefighters in a position of needing basic first aid training, which evolved with time into the more advanced Emergency Medical Technician training. Now firefighters could care for the patient before the ambulance arrived.

As time progressed, the fire service stepped up to the plate and began to train some of their firefighters to the most advanced level of prehospital medical care: that of the paramedics. This ensures that folks who call 911 get the highest level of medical care available until the ambulance arrives. In many metropolitan areas ambulance companies arrive with their own paramedics to continue the care already begun by the firefighters, taking over the responsibility of transporting the patient to the hospital. The fire engine is then available for the next call for help. In some cases fire departments even have their own ambulances. In short, we've gone from hand-pulled water pumpers to highly trained medical personnel with the most advanced equipment in the world in only a few generations.

Our journey continued as Dan worked, reviewed, applied, and interviewed, with me by his side as a somewhat reluctant accomplice. The encouragement and support I wanted to offer were at odds with my overwhelming desire to control the events of our future by nudging him into a career that was a little more predictable and safe. But feelings of concern were never able to really take hold, as I saw the look of defeat spread across his face each time he opened a letter of rejection. My desire to encourage him into another line of work was replaced by a desire to help him. I felt determined to help my husband get the job I knew he so deeply desired.

It seemed implausible that such an honest and hard-working man could be turned down so many times. Could there really be that many firefighters looking for work? The answer was yes. Dan was applying at a time when the market was saturated with applicants. In many cases hundreds of men and women were applying for only two or three positions. I was crestfallen when I saw how hard he worked only to be turned down. But I was alone with my pity, as the rejections seemed only to spur him on. Setting his jaw like flint, he continued to apply.

He had all but exhausted his search for a job near our home in the San Francisco Bay Area, and began setting his sights on smaller departments in more rural areas. His career pursuit was beginning to affect our lives, as Dan drove farther and farther away to apply.

He applied in Petaluma, a town fifty miles north of San Francisco in the heart of the wine country and two and a half hours from our home in the East Bay. It was a small department, only three stations, but it had an aggressive paramedic program and was well versed in some of the specialty training that came with Dan's résumé. His swift-water rescue experience might be useful, given the river that runs along the edge of town. High-angle rescue opportunities could be afforded by stretches of jagged coastline that were frequented by hikers. Even with such options, the town was rural enough to bring with it the false hope that the risks would be limited.

There were pros and cons to be considered. The town was quaint and historic, which was a nice way of saying old, and most of the firefighters were locals, which meant the department had an air of exclusiveness about it. It was intimidating enough trying to break into a large department; with a smaller department, hiring could be more selective and discriminating. This often left applicants feeling as if they were competing for a membership to an elitist club.

Unfortunately, I knew some of this firsthand, as Petaluma was one of the smaller towns in an area I had grown up in. Sensing the constraints that small-town U.S.A. would have on my dreams, I had moved to the East Bay to work and live in a more metropolitan area. My determination to support my husband's career faltered in the face of his going to work in a place that I had tried so hard to escape. I was a self-diagnosed city girl now, with a career of my own. I didn't relish the idea of my husband going to work in a town whose claim to fame was as the Chicken Capital of the World. For me, the con list severely outweighed the pro list, which had only one thing on it: the department was hiring.

As far as I was concerned, we were fine where we were.

Ten years after becoming a paramedic, I had left the streets for an educational role and was perfectly content with the direction my life was heading. But the fire department application was in and accepted, and Dan began the process of learning all he could about the place where he had applied. Suddenly he was spending his days off visiting the stations, driving around the countryside preparing himself mentally for the first portion of the process, the written test. More than a hundred candidates showed up for the test, and only the top fifty scorers would be invited back to compete in the physical agility test. After taking more than twenty written tests in the last few years, Dan did well and continued on in the process.

The physical agility was an intense day of testing that included an exhausting array of hands-on exercises to assess his upper-body strength, coordination, and communication skills. One test took the participant to the top of an eighty-five-foot ladder to weed out those with a bit of acrophobia (fear of heights). Freeze on this portion of the testing and you're gone.

There were hose lays and drags to perform, which require the pulling, lifting, and stacking of the two-and-a-half-inch hoses that could be used any time they were fighting a fire. This tested the firefighter candidate's upper-body strength and coordination, but also endurance. There was a seventy-five-pound gurney to carry up and down three flights of stairs with one hundred and fifty pounds added to it, to simulate the rescue of victims from buildings. Not to mention lifting twenty-four-foot ladders on and off the engines without banging the expensive, meticulously maintained equipment.

There would be a chance to demonstrate his familiarity with the various tools used in emergencies. One drill required the would-be firefighters to hold a HURST tool (or "the jaws of life," as it's commonly known) several feet above the ground while putting the tool through its paces. An inability to hold this ninety-pound device until the exercise was completed would disqualify a candidate.

Much to his relief, Dan returned home exhausted but elated, having passed every test. The first two hurdles were behind him.

Next was the part of the process dreaded by most candidates: the panel interview. Consisting of a group of three or four line firefighters (those doing the job) and officers (those who supervise and direct the work), the panel puts the would-be employees through a series of scenarios in an effort to assess the candidate's knowledge base, decision-making skills, and integrity. This is also the time for the auditioner to sell himself or herself, highlighting any qualities, education, or experience that could set him or her ahead of the competitors.

Dan stood nervously before the full-length mirror

checking every inch of his suit. Shirt smooth, no tuck marks? Tie straight? Shoes shined? Check, check, check. We reviewed the questions he anticipated might be asked and rechecked the sheet of facts he'd made about the department's history and details of the community they served. He was ready.

He hated this part of the testing. Being moderately shy and self-effacing made the "selling himself" portion of the interview a huge struggle. He was determined to do well, though, and did the best he could. He gave the panel the facts of what he'd done and where he'd been without embellishment, assuring them that if chosen for the job he would give them everything he had.

It wasn't enough. The department was hiring only four men this time and Dan had been rated number five. The rating itself was an accomplishment in light of the fact that he was competing against dozens of other qualified folks, but it was not enough to get him the job.

We sat together reviewing the letter, which gave him his rating with the minor encouragement that he'd come very close to getting a job offer. That's when I saw him truly discouraged for the first time. He raked his hands through his prematurely thinning crew cut and shook his head. "I did the best I could," he sighed. "If it was meant to be it would have happened." My heart broke for him, but I knew him well enough to realize he wasn't looking for my pity.

"Dan," I said, standing up from the kitchen table, "they don't know what they're missing."

I rummaged through the refrigerator to choose something for lunch as Dan stood and stretched to free himself from the constraint of rejection, saying almost absently, "Well, it's not over till it's over. Those four guys still have to pass their background exams and anything can happen." It felt like waiting for a relative to die to get an inheritance, but it's true: everyone has to complete the entire process before the deal is made. Applicants can be eliminated for poor job reviews from former employers, dishonest answers, information revealed after the interview, or any number of things from their past. They can also be taken off the list for failing to pass a detailed medical exam or psychiatric profile that's given to each finalist. The more you know about the great hoops candidates jump through, the more it begins to sound like a Miss America Pageant. The only thing missing is the swimsuit competition.

The good news was that Dan was on the short list, which meant there was a possibility he would eventually get an offer for employment. But there was the very real chance the list would expire before waiting candidates got their chance, requiring applicants to reapply after a predetermined time. It was a frustrating experience and one that was sure to test the determination and motivation of the candidates.

Weeks went by and the sting of rejection faded. There was a whole future of other adventures ahead of us as we waited and prepared for the arrival of our first child. Dan was content in his job as a paramedic supervisor, and the flexible schedule that came with seniority. We settled into a comfortable routine as our due date grew closer. I was actually a little relieved that Dan had not gotten a fire department job offer in the last few months. That would have put him squarely at the bottom of the totem pole of seniority, guaranteeing that he would have no time off when our new baby arrived. The rejection was a blessing in disguise.

Do you have any idea how hard it is to get the body of a heavily pregnant woman out of the corner of a springless, fifteen-year-old, burnt-orange, corduroy sectional sofa? We should have replaced the sofa before I was pregnant, but who could have known the effect forty pounds in seven months could have on one's ability to get up from a sitting position? I heaved myself out of the pit I had created in my favorite part of the couch and waddled to the phone, panting as if I'd sprinted across town to answer it.

"Hellllllooo?" I queried, expecting the voice of my mother-in-law, who was checking daily on the progress of the transporting device for her first grandchild.

"Hello, Mrs. Farren, I suppose?"

"Yes," I answered cautiously, expecting the telemarketer spin to begin.

"This is Chief Simpson from the Petaluma Fire Department. Is Dan available?"

My heart began to pound as each word found its way from his mouth to my ear. The fire department!

"Just a second, please."

"Daaaannnn!" I half screamed, hustling my girth to the front yard, where Dan was intently mowing symmetrical lines into our lawn. "It's a chief from the Petaluma Fire Department!" I thrust the phone into his hand, trying to suppress the excitement that wanted to spill all over me.

"Yes, Chief, this is Dan," he said, plugging one ear and beginning to pace across his newly mowed lines. "Yes, sir . . . okay . . . yes, sir . . . I'll do what I can, sir . . ." Snippets of his end of the conversation held me hostage as I tried to keep up with his pacing, animatedly mouthing and gesturing, "What are they saying? What, what, what?"

The pacing stopped as Dan clicked the phone off and turned to me with a look of shock and amazement. "What?" I cried, ready to go into labor from the suspense.

"The guy in first place on the list failed his physical. I've been moved up the list and they want to know if I can start the training academy next week."

I whooped and hollered until I cried, hugging my new fireman as closely as one can with another human between them. "I knew you could do it," I wept. The preparing, praying, and waiting were finally coming to an end.

Little did I know that the preparing, praying, and waiting were only the first step in the process of becoming a
firefighter. The whole journey from application to employment was beginning to have an eerie resemblance to my
pregnancy. How was I to know the real labor of his job was
about to begin?

It is seven and a half years before my husband's accident.

MARRIED TO THE MOB

～

"Wives may come and go, but the department will always be here for you; we're your second family now."

Dan was thrilled to hear these words spoken to him by one of his new colleagues his first day on the job, thrilled with the idea of having a second family, thrilled to tell me the news.

All I could think was, "Oh goody, my husband has just gone to work for 'The Firm.'"

I began reconsidering how thankful I was that Dan had finally landed the job. Pending his survival of the eighteen-month probationary phase, he would soon be a full-fledged firefighter. I got an eerie sensation that when that happened

I would no longer be married just to Dan, but to an entire department as well.

My first clue was that his coworkers were referred to as "brothers." In other words, our future children would be inheriting sixty new uncles—men who would be more than delighted to wrestle with them, love them, let them play on the fire engines, and subtly groom them to follow in their father's footsteps. No need to recruit firefighters if we can reproduce them, after all.

Oh, please, God, give me girls!

After his first couple of shifts Dan brought me in to meet the guys he worked with and to give me a tour of the place where he would be spending half his life without me. The firefighters were a nice and, dare I say, eclectic bunch. They had some similarities, of course. Besides the obvious commitment to hard work and self-sacrifice, they wore the same uniforms and in some cases had remarkably similar moustaches. But there the commonalities seemed to end. Some of the firefighters were amazingly outgoing and friendly; others appeared almost sullen and detached, wary of the new guy. There were the quiet, introspective ones sitting next to those who appeared to be auditioning for the comedy circuit with their constant barrage of sarcasm and jokes. There was the guy who was working on his degree in holistic medicine adjacent to the guy who was rummaging through the bottom of a pink box in hopes of finding the last bits of a chocolate éclair (his third of the day). Some of the men were exceedingly athletic, competing in triathlons and fire department Olympics; others were content to watch them, keeping the recliners warm.

There was the guy with the beautiful baritone voice who sang as he went from room to room as well as the guy they all prayed would *stop* singing. The educated and articulate worked side by side with the experienced and opinionated. Some were amazing and others just odd. But in spite of their quirks and differences, the united commitment to one another and the people they served gave the firehouse the air of a family reunion.

The men were, by and large, extremely polite and helpful, going out of their way to make me feel welcome in the family. If their schedules afforded them a few minutes they gladly joined us, helping Dan show me around the station. They took pride in introducing me to the different parts of their home away from home.

The more experienced escort made sure to point out the interesting and unique parts of the department and equipment, as if maybe I were in the market to buy the place. It made me nervous to see Dan standing there beaming at me as if I were a Stepford wife as his "brother" gave me the hard sell on the terrific department he'd just joined. Unconsciously I had the fear that the lure and excitement of his new job and home would somehow lure him away from me. The tour guide sensed my uncertainty. As a man who'd seen many a wife struggle with the transition into the fire service, he knew to assure me with great humor that my husband would not disappear into a firefighting vortex. He had merely become part of a team.

I couldn't imagine how I was going to adjust to this new life with a man who would spend an unwelcome portion of his life away from home, a man who would, at times, be asked to run into burning buildings for a living. The living that would allow him to live some of his life with me might require that he give his life for others.

But as I saw him in this new environment, in his element, I realized being a firefighter wasn't just something he chose to do, it was more like something he was *born* to do. He was exactly where he wanted to be. I might have succeeded in convincing him to do something other than this, but he would always have longed for the missing part of himself, this career and second family he was meant to be a part of.

No matter that at the moment the family appeared to be a bit more like the Sopranos than the Waltons.

Our chaperone, called away to the phone, allowed Dan to pick up the last leg of the tour like an excited real estate agent. His enthusiasm and pride were infectious as I surrendered to the feeling of being inside, and minutely a part of, the hallowed halls that up until now I had only read about. It's an environment that few people get to see except on TV, or on a field trip.

The unveiling included the perfunctory, which involved a peek into the locker that held his brand-new crisply pressed uniform, complete with the nostalgia and confines of every high-school locker in America. Other lockers, some left open for convenience, revealed family photos, vacation mementos, and handmade artwork from kids or field trip fans. The lockers would hold the standard fare of toiletries and changes of clothing, but, I learned, might also store the hidden treasure of favored candy, coffee, or snacks, which were supposedly off limits to the other firefighters. Apparently many a practical joke would be given life in the confines of this room.

The sleeping quarters, maintained at the end of a cool hallway with cement floors, appeared to be little more than a great room with cubicle dividers separating what looked like government-issue military beds. The firefighters' preferred beds were clearly staked out with personal belongings, sleeping bags, and pillows.

There were separate sleeping areas for women and officers, and they even had a snoring room for the guy who shakes the walls when he sleeps. Dan said the snoring room was for the comfort of the other firefighters, but a small wink told me it was for the safety of the snorer, lest the other men smother him for keeping them awake. Sleep was apparently a highly prized commodity for the firefighters, considering that most of their nights were spent running calls. Dan pointed out the speakers that sounded with electronic tones when a call came in, followed by the soft-spoken voice of a dispatcher giving the details. In the past, the first sound a fireman might hear would have been more of a bell or gong, but departments have long since eliminated these jangling alarms, as their intensity added to the stress of the nighttime calls.

Our shoes squeaked on the recently waxed floors as we viewed training rooms and offices, which constant maintenance kept uncluttered. With the exception of bookshelves filled with firefighting manuals and training videos—and officers' desks with overflowing boxes—the station felt almost sparse. The hallways and rooms possessed a sort of echo-chamber quality that made me want to whisper, something which the firefighters probably did very seldom.

Beyond the lockers, restrooms, and sleeping quarters there was very little that could be considered personal at the firehouse. The reading areas and training rooms could be used for quiet work or study, but everywhere else communal living was the rule.

A heavy wooden door that groaned when Dan opened it gave way to a large day room, the second most popular room in the house. It would be in this room that Dan and the other firefighters would spend most of their time when not running calls or doing housework. A large unused pool table sat at one side of the room, covered by moss-green particleboard edged with white lines—a makeshift Ping-Pong table. Unopened mail, a disheveled stack of blank forms, a mostly empty box of pastries, and a forgotten jacket littered the unused surface. Shiny, well-worn red and black squares of linoleum rested beneath a wide semicircle of recliners, poised around the major source of conversation, rivalry, and entertainment, the TV. Dan said that although most of the stations had pool tables, Ping-Pong tables, or exercise equipment, the TV was still the most common gathering place when the firefighters had a few minutes of down time.

An area that was as much a part of the life of the station as the day room was the apparatus bay. A cavernous garage with twenty-foot ceilings, painted floors, and huge rolling doors, the bay housed all of the enormous firefighting equipment. The size of this room guaranteed that the engines and trucks rarely came and went without everyone else in the station knowing it.

I slowly made my way around the beautifully maintained equipment, marveling at the polished chrome of gauges and dials that were used only by those who understood them and were strong enough to turn them. I was intimidated by the daunting size of the vehicles, something that became apparent when Dan offered to let me climb into the cab of an engine. A surprisingly delicate *click* released the door that dared me to make the climb up to the driver's seat and perch my pregnant body in a position higher than even the tallest SUV. I settled into what felt like a wide-bottomed leather throne, awestruck at the sea of glass before me, more like a plate-glass window than any windshield I'd ever seen. Driving a fire engine, I realized, would be more like driving a living room than a vehicle. Being in a fire engine reminded me of the sensation I'd had standing at the edge of the Grand Canyon. All the postcards and photos in the world couldn't prepare me for the enormity of the environment until I stood at the canyon's edge. It brought me another burst of respect for those who appeared to navigate these devices through busy streets so effortlessly, even with lights and sirens blaring.

I thought about the bumper stickers I'd seen: "The difference between men and boys is the size of their toys." The "large" pickup truck bearing that sticker brought a smile to my face. Would the firemen even bother to snicker as they shadowed such Tonka toys? Those playthings that pretended to be the rulers of the road until they were brushed aside by the real road kings?

I donned the cushioned headset and listened as Dan, sitting in a seat that backed up against my own, explained how these earphones made hearing possible over the roar of the engines.

I was nine years old again as I gripped the steering wheel, the size of one of the tires on my minivan. I imagined the thrill and terror of driving to my first fire. Dan smiled as he helped me down from the elevated seat and saw the awe on my face. I wandered, speechless, stopping momentarily to stare up at the gleaming pole, which stood silently behind the engine. The sign on the wall beside it (meant only for visitors) initially seemed to provide a dilemma had it been meant for the firefighters: PLEASE DON'T TOUCH THE BRASS POLE. Dan, seeing my confusion, explained how the pole was used for expedience for the firefighters coming down from the second floor and that fingerprints made the pole sticky and slow. I stopped just short of asking if I could slide down it.

Before my tour came to its predictable end I was escorted through one of the most important parts of every firehouse in America: the kitchen.

This is, I was told, where everything that sustained, encouraged, and comforted the firefighters was created. The countertops were void of typical kitchen accoutrements and gave way to the biggest stove/oven combination I had ever seen in my life. Cast-iron pans hung at the ready above a large, constantly-in-use, two-potted coffee machine that offered up the last remnants of the morning's caffeine jumpstart.

There was a hominess and nostalgia here that eluded

the rest of the department. More important, I realized the kitchen would be part of my husband's training ground. Yee-haw, Dan was going to learn how to cook! The resident experts would gladly take a new recruit under their wing and teach him the ropes. The adage that the way to a man's heart is through his stomach still holds true in firehouses today. But as with a favorite firehouse joke—"How many shrinks does it take to change a lightbulb? One, but the lightbulb has to really want to change"—it takes more than a good teacher to become a firehouse cook. The firemen were willing to teach him to cook, but he had to want to learn; they wouldn't force him over the stove. Experience had taught them well: add a man who doesn't want to cook to a man who doesn't like to cook, and you'll get food you don't want to eat. The resident chefs do their best to keep those guys out of the kitchen, as there's plenty of other work to keep them occupied. Lucky for me, Dan was interested.

Dan would humbly minimize the efforts he and the other cooks made by saying that the only recipe at the firehouse is "Make it hot and make a lot." But sticking around long enough to have dinner with the shift revealed that it wasn't mush they were serving. The guys were marinating meats, making sauces, creating fabulous salads, and downright spoiling each other. Food at the firehouse is a source of nutrition, comfort, and conversation, but also of tough competition and the unspoken delight of making new recipes and acquiring the most compliments. Their talents and creations are sometimes made known to the public at fire department chili cookoffs, BBQs, and fundraisers. Then there is the more direct link of simply marrying one of the cooks. The former come with fewer struggles than the latter, as once the new firefighters learn how to cook, their wives apparently forget. As for me, tried-and-true techniques of the firehouse—everything from the cast-iron pans to the temperatures they use, hot and fast for almost everything—would eventually find their way into my kitchen.

The high quality of firehouse cooking is, in part, due to the freshness of the food. Every firefighter who wants to participate in the house meals puts money into a kitty, an account that's used for the day's purchases. The men who are in charge of cooking do the shopping between calls, which is why you can find them in grocery stores every day. They purchase their supplies, smile at the grateful public, and try to make it back to the station before getting called out again.

If the firefighters are fortunate enough to make it to the store and back in time to cook, their coworkers are the lucky ones. It's my opinion that some of the best food in the country is served in firehouses. It's a well-deserved luxury for these men and women, who aren't guaranteed they'll get to do anything more than smell the food cooking before the tones go off, leaving them with nothing more than the world's best leftovers.

The real devotion to food with firefighters became more apparent when Dan heard, over one of his first meals, that food preparation isn't only a part of daily life, but can also be a kind of penalty. Rookie and seasoned firefighters alike are aware of the expectations. Having an action photo or unplanned quote in the paper means buying ice cream for the entire shift (and every station in smaller departments). Get interviewed or *pose* for a photo, and the ante is raised to steak for everyone. Successfully complete probation and you can expect to cook the entire shift dinner. Take a promotion, take your crew *out* to dinner. The ever-popular retirement dinner will include good food, plenty of drinks, and hours of retelling stories and embarrassing moments of the retiree. Although different departments have different traditions, most of them revolve around food.

After an afternoon and evening of being introduced to the firehouse, Dan's new family, some firehouse food, and an insider's view of a few of the firehouse traditions, I went away with my appetite sated, my apprehension mollified, my curiosity satisfied, and my excitement and pride renewed. These feelings would come and go over the rest of my days as a fireman's wife, but it was wonderful to bask in them for the moment.

THE PROBIES

⌒

AFTER DAN AND THE other new recruits were put through an "academy," a multiweek training period familiarizing them with department procedures and equipment, came a period of time referred to as "probation." During this time the new recruits will be trained and supervised by a combination of firefighters and company officers they work with. Collectively they will evaluate if the candidate possesses the right attitude and skills to perform the job and become part of the team. Concerns and recommendations will be forwarded to the chief, who will have the final say over the career of the future firefighter. The candidates are well aware that they are expected to be putting their best foot forward every time they show up for work. As the wife of a probationary firefighter, this time seemed a bit more like fire department adultery. I watched my husband prepare for work each shift as if he were going to meet a mistress, taking extra care with his uniform and personal appearance to ensure he was sending a message on every level that this job mattered to him.

Most of the expectations for Dan's probation were clear, the standards written or spoken. But there were vitally important parts that weren't in writing. They were the intangibles, the things you couldn't put your finger on, but they were as real as anything documented. It was the intuitive part of the job, the part every fireman understood and none could explain. Probation is about who belongs, who fits in, and who is "cut from the cloth," as firemen say. With enough hard work and a clear understanding of what's wanted, some could fake it for a period of time. But the job seemed to be easier for those who were born with the firefighting microchip already installed. Those are the folks who seem to have what it takes naturally. They get the hard work, the humor, and the occasionally quirky personalities; they mesh right in without disturbing the firehouse's delicate infrastructure.

More than anything, I saw how important it was that the men got along. This included the recruits' ability to take a verbal beating now and then. The men each had their own way of teaching, and the new recruits were rotated through all the stations for the men to get a feel for them and be given a chance to offer them their own twist on the job. Some of the men preferred to teach by example, and others simply delighted in the opportunity to hear themselves talk. No matter what the probationary firefighters thought of their mentors, they knew better than to have an opinion. It was best to smile and nod and take each piece of advice without commenting. Early into this process the firemen would be forming an opinion of the new recruit and gathering information about their likes, dislikes, education, and hobbies. Once the recruits' weaknesses and strengths are revealed, the games begin.

Dan would tell me stories of firemen, notorious for their sometimes warped senses of humor, indoctrinating the new guys around the dinner table. This is the time when one of the firemen will bring up a detail—like the fact that a recruit is from a really small town—and ask them how much of the population they're related to. A good recruit will see this coming and play along without missing a beat, or even let the fireman get a good laugh at his expense. He knows he's only biding his time until his probation status ends and he is eligible to participate in the game.

The unspoken expectations are never far from the surface, and all those who are being considered for future full-time employment stay on their toes, striving to do everything in their power to meet or exceed the expectations that most of them know exist.

There was a written expectation to be on time for work; the unspoken expectation was to be more than half an hour early. The written expectation was that they would pull their share of the load; the unspoken expectation was that they would go the extra mile, always be willing to do more than their share. It was expected of the recruits to be motivated, hard-working, and pleasant to work with. The unspoken extra credit was to keep the coffeepot full, fresh, and made early. It never hurt to make sure your shift had their fill of fresh morning pastries, either. When overtime became available they could display their eagerness not just by their willingness to sign up but also by being first on the list.

Probation would separate the front-line firefighters from those who were still proving themselves. The freedom to enjoy a meal, combined with a few minutes to rest or watch TV, was reserved for those who had already survived probation. The new recruits were the last to sit down and the first to get up from a meal to offer to clean up. Downtime would rarely find them resting, watching TV, or talking on the phone, as they would be expected to be studying, practicing their skills, and familiarizing themselves with equipment. It would be the recruits who would be first to the phones and doorbells during the day, and the first to the engines and ambulances in the middle of the night. It was not just their skills that were being watched, but also their attitudes—their eagerness, their willingness to please.

There was a part of me that understood this and a part of me that despised it. But the departments did not want to make a mistake. The people they hired were in many cases making career commitments; they might never leave or transfer departments. Failing to identify a difficult personality or someone who would not be committed to teamwork could be a burden for the entire department for many years to come. It became apparent that this was going to be the most difficult phase of the job, not just for my husband but for me as well. During this time he had to remind me on a regular basis that the department's needs had to come first. His days of seniority would come eventually if I would just be patient.

It was during this difficult time that our first son, Benjamin, arrived. I was dreading the impact my husband's probationary status was going to have on our family, knowing that he'd accrued no time off in the two months he'd been there. This had been the primary reason I was so grateful he hadn't gotten a job offer during my pregnancy. (Or that was the excuse I was using at this moment.)

On the day of Benjamin's arrival I was as predictably overwhelmed as a first-time mother could be. Compound it with the fact that Dan would be going back to work the following morning for a forty-eight-hour shift, and the resentment I had already begun to secretly foster became harder to handle. Deep down inside I was ashamed of my thoughts. I knew that women all over the world give birth with husbands away on assignment in the military or without husbands at all. But I had only my life's experience to contend with, and wanted my husband beside me.

The disappointment would be short-lived, though. The true nature of the fire department was revealed as we arrived home. There was a beautiful bouquet of flowers waiting on our porch with a personal sentiment from the firefighters' union, a union my husband was not yet a part of because of his probationary status. The flowers were followed by a phone call from the chief to discuss my husband's time-off status—or, more accurately, the fact that he didn't have any coming. It turned out that the senior firefighters were all too aware of the struggles of probationary life on the new families. It was, unbeknownst to me, a common practice for the senior guys to help out new recruits in our situation. This became apparent when one of the officers, Captain Nockleby, unexpectedly donated more than two hundred hours of his accrued vacation time to an account for Dan, so he could be home with his wife and new son. Dan's chance to return the favor would come in time as he stepped up to the plate to cover when the senior men wanted special trades or time off. It was just another part of the unwritten rules of brotherhood. I was grateful beyond words and began to see more clearly how the invisible and unspoken parts of the job were so important. Maybe this career wasn't going to be so painful after all.

TINY GENIUS

We marveled at each tiny breath. Every squeak, grunt, or miniature movement would be met with some version of "Oh, honey, come quick, look what he's doing now!" There was every indication this child would grow up to be a genius, or so thought his slack-jawed, wide-eyed parents. But after two and a half idyllic weeks of staring into the face of our new miracle, Dan was going to have to go back to work. I was suddenly alone with the tiny genius, who woke every hour and a half to be fed or changed.

Dan and I began comparing stories of who had been up more often the night before to determine who would get the first nap. It drew a new thread of understanding between us, as the career of firefighting paralleled that of motherhood. Tensions were high those first few weeks as we competed for the best sleep deprivation stories. Dan ultimately won out, because he actually had to get dressed and leave the station every time he woke up.

As the baby slowly adjusted to the human sleep cycle, my stories of colic and diaper blowouts began to wane, replaced by expectation. I kept hoping Dan would come home rested, eager to hear the stories of a woman who was alone all day and night with a drooling, cooing, burping, crying creature who couldn't communicate. But so many of his days home were spent recovering. He would take a few minutes to marvel at the changes he saw in the baby he had left only forty-eight hours earlier and worry some about the changes he saw in me. But he was gracious enough to listen, keep his concerns about me to himself, and give a hand with the chores I seemed unable to keep up with since the baby's arrival. He would take a few minutes to give me a general rundown of his shift as I sat on the edge of my seat, hungry for word of the outside world. He tried to comply with as much detail as he could remember, before I was predictably interrupted by the genius's dirty diaper or hungry mouth. It took me away just long enough for Dan to fall asleep on the sofa.

Dan's life at the firehouse required him to work a Kelly schedule, which had him working a tour of duty. This consisted of one day on, one day off, three times in a row, followed by four days off. The easiest way to see it was to play it out in my head or, more embarrassingly, count it out on my fingers to see if we were available on a particular day. One on, one off, one on, one off, one on, four off, the constantly rotating schedule never allowing the same days off every week. But four days off in a row would be the most coveted and necessary part of the schedule, which would allow Dan to fully recover from his tour.

At the outset it appeared like a terrific schedule, with an average month taking him away only ten to twelve days. But they were not just days—they were twenty-four-hour shifts. There would be no mandated coffee breaks, lunch hours, or sleep schedules. If the calls came in, the firefighters went, any moment of the day or night. Calls would most predictably come at meal time or bedtime, leaving the firefighters joking that the dispatchers could hear a fork touch a plate or a head hit a pillow.

The shift life Dan lived put each man in a category—A, B, or C shift. A C shift firefighter working overtime on an A shift would still be referred to as a C-shifter. The individual shift assignments created a unique camaraderie as the men adjusted to living with the same group of guys in the same houses and on the same shifts for months or years. Changes in shifts happened incrementally, as new faces came in and the older ones retired or firefighters went out injured. But no matter how many people came and went, there was always going to be a unique sense of commitment and loyalty to the shift.

This shift life is completely separate from anything that takes place at home. With the inside practical jokes and humor being just another part of their life together, each shift has its own reputation and fodder—A shift could be known for running the most fires, earning them credit as a "bad-luck magnet," while C shift might be known for having the most aggressive and boisterous firefighters, "the loud crowd," as it were. But B shift—well, B shift seemed to have its own unique reputation. At the outset I thought this might be something of an insider's joke at Dan's department, but as we met folks in the fire service from all over the country I discovered the reputation was universal. "Better to have a sister in a brothel than a brother on B shift" was muttered in firehouses the country over, insinuating there was some type of attitude change the moment a firefighter was placed on this shift. Of course the statement had no authentic bearing on the quality of the people who worked B shift and came with a note of caution. Shifts could be rotated based on departmental needs, and the C-shifter who had dared to whisper this line could find himself a B-shifter in the blink of an eye.

I gave up trying to figure out all the nuances of what took place in the firehouse and was content to just have

Dan come home. But my optimism was dampened the first few times he walked through the door smelling like smoke. He didn't need to say a word; if he smelled like fire, he'd been fighting one, which meant he hadn't slept.

I had to give up making plans for him on his days off when I discovered that even on the nights when they didn't fight fire Dan never really rested, no matter how hard he tried to sleep. The environment keeps them alert, ready at a moment's notice, preventing any of them from ever sleeping too soundly.

The exhaustion of fighting fires at night was followed closely by the weariness he felt after long nights running medical aids on the ambulance. The best thing I could hope to hear when he came home was that he'd only had to do a "trucker's roll," nights when dispatch tones meant the ambulance was leaving and the men assigned to the truck needed only to roll over and go back to sleep.

It was an adjustment to learn that all of our postshift plans would have to be tentative, as Dan found the balance between his family off duty and his family on duty. The dedication and commitment he had to his home life would regularly have to be tempered with the needs of this department.

At times his new job required him to spend more time with his new brothers than with me, relegating me to one half of a life that was lived on two entirely different fronts. Our home life together wasn't disconnected from the firehouse life, it was incorporated with it. Important conversations would still take place between us, but some of them would have to take place over the phone. I was enormously self-conscious of the fact that the other firemen could sometimes hear his end of our discussions. More than once I would find myself pleading, "You're not saying this in front of the other firemen, are you?" Too often I got the nonchalant response of "Oh, honey, they're not listening anyway."

It seems there wasn't a topic of conversation between husbands and wives that hadn't been heard at least once, over the years, by the rest of the department. Even the unmarried guys would become amateur therapists, learning about the art of marriage around the dining room table. I was, quite frankly, a little leery of the firemen becoming aware of facets of our lives reserved only for immediate family and close friends. But that's just because I wasn't yet aware that these folks were part of my immediate family.

There was the added frustration of being interrupted in the middle of some of these important phone calls by tones that were always followed by the words, "I've gotta go." *Click*. Leaving me once again with an empty phone line, an incomplete thought, and nobody but a mute genius with a dirty diaper to talk to. This life was going to take a lot of patience on my part.

STOP, DROP, AND ROLL

"OH, MY, YOU'RE MARRIED to a firefighter? Don't you worry about him? Doesn't it bother you that he goes into burning buildings and risks his life every day? I mean, he could be killed at any moment! How do you handle it?"

I stood there, surrounded by a cornucopia of fruits and vegetables, a smile plastered across my face. The melon I had been thumping only moments ago was forgotten as I instinctively clutched the front pack on my chest shielding my sleeping three-month-old son from the painful reality about his daddy's job. I tried to say something casual, like, "Well, I try not to worry too much about that part of the job," all the while suppressing the desire to speed-dial Dan's cell phone and beg him to turn in his resignation.

Realistically speaking, Dan doesn't risk his life every time he goes to work. Some of his shifts are quite mundane, in fact. He may not do much more than business inspections, training, dousing a Dumpster fire, or performing a few minor medical aids. There are always folks, however, who imagine his job as being constantly on the cutting edge of danger, folks who, with no malice intended, are eager to share that disastrous vision with me.

It wasn't like I could avoid people finding out what he did for a living. One of the unanticipated consequences of being married to a firefighter is the acquisition of fire-related accessories. Home décor (wall plates, pictures, figurines, throw blankets, jewelry, checkbooks, calendars, and the like), vehicle stickers, personalized license plates, and articles of clothing (T-shirts and ball caps for the adults, pajamas, onesies, and fireman outfits for the baby) all seemed to worm their way into our life. Gifts we received for any occasion took on a particular firefighting theme. The baby's dangling Dalmatian-clad legs happened to be the catalyst for the most recently asked questions. And although they might deny it, I think the firemen wear the T-shirts so they can spot each other in a crowd and spend just a few more minutes talking shop, much to the consternation of their wives. But I digress.

The truth is, I was worried. Dan's job wasn't always at the forefront of my mind, but it was a very real part of my life. Not the what-will-I-tell-my-mother-in-law-if-she-asks-where-the Christmas-gift-from-last-year-is kind of worry. It was more like the feeling you get when your child is late coming home. The how-will-I-handle-it-if-something-terrible-happens kind of worry. Except the worry seemed to loiter for twenty-four hours at a time, or whatever the length this week's shift might be. I worried about his safety, I worried about his health, and I worried about the toll the job was taking on him. I worried for me, I worried for our son, and I worried that I was worrying too much. It felt like the fire department should be writing me a check for all the work I was doing worrying.

I was aware that worry was a part of being alive, but as the wife of a new fireman there were times when I felt terribly alone with my fear. The circle of friends who could relate to my life seemed to evaporate when he embarked on this career. I tried telling myself that I should somehow be able to handle Dan's job without thinking about the risks. I reminded myself that I was not the only one in this situation. Families of police officers and soldiers know this struggle, too, probably in a much deeper way in some cases. It's an invisible thread that ties us all together.

I imagine that the families of plumbers and bankers have their sorts of worries, too (no offense to plumbers and bankers intended), but it's not the same kind of thing. I can't imagine that every time one of them leaves for work their spouse thinks it may be the last time they will see them.

It was the worry, then, that prompted me into reciting the same words every time he left: "I love you, be safe, you're my best friend," the words I prayed he remembered, and the routine I hoped would somehow protect him.

So it was most days. My parting words spoken, I would go on about my business without allowing the what-ifs to follow me around. But on the occasions I mentioned to someone what my husband did for a living—and they responded with a telltale line of innocent, albeit disconcerting, questions or comments—the animal reared its head, the animal that left me wanting to scurry for protection from the reality of the risks—the risk Dan would be injured or killed every time he responded to a dangerous call.

I do mental gymnastics to focus on the wonderful parts of his job. I remind myself that he works with a group of incredibly well-trained people, people who, having no way of knowing what each event may have in store for them, practice and practice to anticipate and avoid unnecessary risks. The same group of people is as concerned with Dan's well-being as they are with their own, being inclined to risk their lives for one another before counting the cost to themselves. That fact both comforts and terrifies me, as Dan is just as committed to doing the same for them.

In retrospect, I guess this information doesn't keep me from worrying—it just comforts me while I'm doing it. There would continue to be a lot of emotions to adjust to over the years. I knew early on that worrying about him was destined to be one of them. I just didn't realize it could sneak up on me in the produce aisle of a grocery store, but life is full of surprises.

911, WHAT'S YOUR EMERGENCY?

WE WERE EIGHT MONTHS into Dan's career when the news that we were expecting a second child brought us to another major decision. Dan was working two and a half hours from home, meaning this would be another pregnancy without him close by. It was time to move.

There were many adjustments to make. I would be giving up my full-time job in the East Bay as a paramedic instructor, and we would be leaving our first home together. Resentment started nibbling at my mind as I dealt with another major transition because of Dan's career. It wasn't going to be an option for Dan to transfer to a department closer to our current home. He had made a commitment to his department and intended to keep it.

Comforting myself with the idea of us being so much closer to his work when he was gone, I agreed somewhat reluctantly to the idea of moving. It would make visiting the firehouse a far more realistic option than it was now, with the five-hour round-trip drive.

There was only one condition: I didn't want to live in the small town just north of Petaluma. I'm not sure why I felt so strongly about it other than it was the last place I had lived before moving to the East Bay and it held some un-pleasant memories—memories of loss and poor personal decisions. We agreed that we would look everywhere else first.

Six months and eighty-six houses later we found our home. It was everything we needed. Nestled in a small cul-de-sac, it had the appearance of an older, comfortably sized cottage that had been kept clean and well maintained. An-tique rosebushes lined a pebbled walkway, inviting visitors to stop and smell the blossoms before continuing up the brick steps to the oversized front door. A comfortable and open floor plan was waiting beyond a small entry that led to a surprisingly spacious backyard, perfect for a growing family.

There was the added bonus of a locally owned shop-ping center only a stroller's walk away, with everything a young mother could possibly need while her husband was gone on extended shifts: a modest grocery store, Laundromat, dry cleaner, pharmacy. Late-night pizza or early morning donuts, too.

But all of these things—a comfortable home, a good-sized backyard, a convenient shopping center, and, the biggest selling point of all, being in our price range—put us smack-dab in the middle of the town I least wanted to live in. Compromise seemed to be another verb I was going to have to get accustomed to.

Six weeks after the arrival of a baby girl we named Bailey (after my much-loved and long-since-departed mother), Dan and I moved into our new home. A fifteen-minute drive to work for Dan and the bonus of a husband who wasn't so far away at night seemed at first to hold the promise of more and better sleep. But it wasn't just distance that kept me from sleeping well. In fact, I felt more vulnerable now, with small children at home.

Several months after our move, I was getting reluctantly accustomed to the idea that no matter where we lived I would not sleep as soundly when Dan was gone.

So when a crashing sound woke me one night, it brought me bolt upright in bed. I was scared and disoriented and unsure of what I'd heard. Was it a window breaking? A door opening? Or was it just a bad dream? My mind was foggy and afraid, leaving me unsure of what to do.

I didn't like this feeling, not just the fear but the vulnerability. I hated that I would be unable to protect the children or myself in Dan's absence. In the short span of single life to motherhood I had exchanged a peaceful night's sleep for a pounding heart, shortness of breath, and sweaty palms in five seconds flat.

My first instinct was to grab the phone and call 911, but the reality of living in the district where Dan works is that he will either hear the call go out—which could freak him out—or he'd hear about it later. Maybe first from somebody in the industry who responded to the call, letting him know that things were okay at home. But after that, he'd hear about it from the guys he works with, over and over again. Just a fun little perk that comes with the territory.

Calling Dan for help or advice isn't an option I want to use in the middle of the night. If he is not out running a call he's trying desperately to get a few moments of undisturbed sleep. Even during daylight hours, there was no guarantee he would be available to take my calls and I didn't want to contribute to the stress of his job anyway. I know he needs to be able to focus, to go on calls without problems at home distracting him from the task at hand. When he's at work he is no longer in a position to be my first line of defense, no matter how nervous I might be.

However, at this moment I wanted desperately to distract him.

Part of my struggle has always been the fear of being the kind of woman who can't change a lightbulb without her husband's help. There was, after all, a time when I felt completely self-reliant. I was a single woman living alone; I even owned a cordless screwdriver. But my, how quickly life changes.

All it took was stepping out of a career that fostered confidence and independence to turn me into a shivering ball of nerves who would just as soon her husband be the one to handle sounds in the middle of the night.

I sometimes try to deceive myself into believing that military wives have it easier. At least on base there is security, MPs, and other women in the same situation nearby. Then again, what do I know? Maybe they're terrified and clinging to their blankets, too.

I'm still sitting here, attached to my moment of madness, my knees drawn up, my blanket tucked tightly under my chin, waiting for another sound, my insecurities swirling around me. Forget my pride and my husband's reputation, I'm calling the police!

But what if I really were to make this call?

"This is 911, what's your emergency?"

"Oh, I, um, thought I heard a sound."

Silence. I can see the dispatcher now, scanning the caller ID and mouthing to his colleagues, "It's the fireman's wife again."

"What kind of sound would that be, ma'am?" he inquires patiently.

"I'm not sure, kind of a thumping, crashing, screeching sound. I think there might be someone in the house."

"Well, ma'am"—there's that word again—"why don't you take a look and we'll stay on the line . . . or would you prefer we send a police car over?"

"Oh, no, that won't be necessary, I, um, let me just get up and look around," I stammer, trying to kick my sheet-bound legs free. For no reason I can identify, I feel more secure just having the 911 operator on the phone. I'm not sure why. As if "Freeze! I've got an operator on the phone and I'm not afraid to use him!" is going to send a terrified perpetrator fleeing from my home.

I tiptoe my way through the house, peering into darkened rooms. My breath comes in faltering gulps as I prepare to ward off the attacker with the phone.

There they are! Jagged pieces of something sprawled across the shower floor. I look above the shower, expecting to see the broken window through which the perpetrator has entered, and realize we don't have a window above the shower. Fingering the evidence, careful not to disrupt the crime scene, I suddenly realize what it is. Sheepishly, I report my findings to the dispatcher

"Oh, my husband's shaving mirror thingy with the suction cups. It, um, fell off the shower wall. I'm okay now."

There it is. The constant reminder of how quickly things change the minute my husband goes back to work. My confidence, security, and self-esteem have been destroyed by a plastic shaving mirror thingy with faulty suction cups.

Maybe I'll wait and call 911 the next time.

WHAT IF

⌒

OVER THE YEARS I've learned that the empty bed comes with more than one source of frustration. There is certainly the fear factor that takes over when I wake in the middle of the night to unfamiliar sounds, but there is also the increasing concern of a more familiar sound: the ringing phone.

Fumbling for the receiver in the middle of the night, I glance at the numbers next to it: 2:03 A.M. Suddenly I remember that Dan is at the firehouse. Oh, no.

I unconsciously steel myself for what I am about to hear. I have prepared myself for this call, beginning with his first shift at the fire department. "Yes?" I blurt out with unmasked concern. Hesitation, a pause, the caller preparing to deliver the worst news of my life. I struggle to sit up and flip on the light beside me.

My mind quickly recites the scenario I've created for "the call." It may be a concerned chief or firefighter letting me know that my husband has been seriously injured. Details are sketchy, can I get to the hospital quickly? I rehearse how I will handle this in the middle of the night. Get my clothes on; find my purse, my car keys, and the diaper bag. Hustle half-asleep, pajama-clad children into the van. Lord, I wish I were more organized. Or should I wake a neighbor to baby-sit? "Please come quickly, I don't have time to explain." I'll call the neighbor. It's best the children sleep, unaware until morning how drastically our lives have been altered. That is, unless it's the other scenario, the one where the call is to let me know the chief and a chaplain are about to arrive at my front door.

How will I respond? Will my years of being a paramedic help me to maintain some sense of control over my emotions? Or will I fall apart? I imagine I'll be fine until I arrive at the hospital and the first firefighter puts his sympathetic arm around me, grateful that his own wife is not hearing this news. Then—then I will unravel. The protective shield I built up in the line of duty has long since been dissolved by the love and compassion I have discovered as a wife and a mother.

My mind wanders, considering the endless possibilities.

What will I do without my precious husband? His faults are quickly forgotten and replaced with the endless memories of laughter and love. How will I possibly get through life as a single mother? Will I have to go to work, my children placed in the care of strangers? Will they remember their daddy, or will he become just the fireman in the photos?

I envision them huddled beside me, staring through tear-filled eyes at a flag-covered casket, numb to the words of comfort spoken around us as bagpipes mourn our loss with "Amazing Grace."

How I wish I didn't have these morbid thoughts, that Dan's career didn't motivate these scenarios to play themselves out. It's embarrassing to think how many times I have placed running shoes on the feet of my imagination and let them sprint down the path of "what if" to every possible tragic end. I suppose it's my mind's way of processing, preparing, and protecting me for the moment I may have to cope with all of this.

But I'm never going to be prepared for this. No matter what happens, I, too, have to take it one step at a time. I think of all the families that have gone before me and try to reassure myself that I will survive. Now is the time to cling to my faith. I know I am not in control of the events surrounding my husband. I may influence our lives by the choices I make, but the final decisions rest in the hands of another.

I am ready. Whatever this call brings, I will face it.

"Yes?" I inquire hesitantly, my voice pleading for reassurance. "Who is this?"

"I'm sorry," I hear from the uncertain voice on the other end of the line, surely afraid to be the one who delivers the news. "I'm afraid I've dialed the wrong number."

Click.

The errant caller will never know he's wakened the wife of a fireman. He will redial without giving his mistake another thought, while I lay awake for half an hour waiting for my heart to resume its normal rate, reflecting on the scenarios that jumped yet again into play. I bury my head under the blankets and try to still the panicked voice inside me. It was, after all, just a wrong number.

HOT COMMODITY

I WOULD ALWAYS WRESTLE with the idea of sharing Dan in some ways and losing him in others, especially when it came to being alone. As I began adjusting to the concerns and issues that permeated our lives, it dawned on me that in all honesty I might be just the tiniest bit jealous of the life Dan led away from home.

All the things that compete for time, attention, or allegiance from the family become suspect in my mind. In the fire service those competitions are doled out on a daily basis as Dan sets off for the other part of his life. I'm mildly jealous of the regular breaks he gets from the constancy of parenting. Not that I don't love being at home with our babies; it's just that the idea of his ability to complete full sentences and finish tasks without the interruption of inquisitive minds and hands seems idyllic to me. He has a break from the distractions that have me unable to remember why I'm standing in a room at any given time throughout the day. How I long to complete a task, any task.

I'm also a little jealous that he goes to a place where people say "Well done" and "Thank you," and pay him while he hears it. I am jealous of the camaraderie, companionship, and respect that are so freely given to him on a regular basis and do not include me. The people he works with are the first ones with him during the difficult calls, as well as the personal victories. They will live through and review the events, calls, and experiences of their day together before he has a chance to call me, having forgotten the details of the story.

I am jealous of the women. Not just the ones whose husbands come home each night, but also the ones who love my husband simply for what he does, the ones who see him only as a knight in shining armor, forgetting that he has habits and weaknesses that make him just a regular guy. I am fearful of their idol worship competing with the level of love and appreciation I show him after becoming accustomed to what he does. He's still our knight in shining armor, but I'm the one who dusts his pedestal.

I am jealous of the cookies, meals, and coffee that seem

to be in a perpetual state of arrival or preparation at the firehouse, the cookies fresh, the food plentiful, and the coffee hot. I am jealous of the fact that he never seems to tire of the men, the job, the antics, and the challenges of the firehouse the way he tires of the fun of his "honey-do" list at home. (Even though I do my best to keep his list in a constant state of flux so he won't get bored with it.)

I am jealous of the laughter, the practical jokes, and the inside humor that knit his brothers together like a well-worn sweater, the way it feels to know he's trying to sound interested in my call when he really wants to get back to the ruckus of rolling dice to see who will wash dishes.

I am jealous of the intimacy, the way the men seem to know each other better than anyone else, knowing one another's strengths and weaknesses. Being at complete odds politically, spiritually, or emotionally one minute, and in complete harmony professionally the next, they are together enough to recognize the nuances that may indicate a brother needs a supportive word, a listening ear, or just a swift kick in the pants. They can push one another's soft spots and come within a hair's breadth of going too far, intuitively aware of who can take a ribbing and who can only give one.

I am jealous of the allegiance that allows them to have a heyday with one another's shortcomings, as if they're members of some secret fraternity, a fraternity with pranks that only they're allowed to play, like dismantling one another's lockers and hiding personal belongings for amusement.

This allegiance also makes them fiercely protective of one another, knowing that the games begin and end with them. I saw this firsthand at a department Christmas party when a new recruit was being molded, shall we say, by some of the veteran firefighters. They were enjoying the opportunity to identify some areas of vanity in the young man's life when an outsider decided to chime in on the conversation. The moment the men realized he was being picked on by someone other than them, the recruit went from being the bait to a brother. The offending outsider was quickly eliminated from the game. It's sort of like traveling with a pack of older brothers around you. They can say and do anything they want, but it's a game only the family can play. My envy of these attributes of the fire family doesn't mean I wish Dan didn't have these opportunities, it's just confessing that I wish I could be more a part of them.

OUT TO LUNCH

⤬

THAT SAID, THERE ARE times when I'm far more involved with the fire department than I would like to be. Those would be the times when they are called to my location for various reasons, some of which I am grateful for and others I would prefer to forget. There was the benefit of having Dan respond to my sister's home when we called 911 after my young niece suffered a seizure. It was wonderful to have Dan and the other firemen we knew and respected caring for her.

But then there was that other time, one I try to forget about, that occurred shortly after our third child arrived. But before I go there, a little background may be helpful.

Our daughter, Bailey, maintained her position as reigning princess in the house as our family was blessed with two more bouncing baby boys, Matthew and Roman. The boys arrived just short of two years from one another. As we rapidly began outnumbering the other firefighters' children at social events and Christmas parties, the most commonly asked question, "Are you done yet?" would be answered by Dan and me the same way: "We don't know."

In the beginning, neither one of us intended to have a large family. But as each child arrived and seemed to uniquely complement the group, there always seemed to be enough space to accommodate just one more. Dan's original intent to have his tubes tied after the arrival of our third ended the moment he stared into the face—a miniature of his own. "Why would we prevent ourselves from having more?" he would say, holding the small bundle moments after his arrival. It was apparent that Matthew was something of a special little guy when we discovered after his delivery that there was a full knot in his umbilical cord. The doctor indicated how fortunate we were that the cord had never grown taut, which would have led to the baby's demise in the last stages of pregnancy. With his name originally planned to be Samuel or Michael, the name Matthew was chosen instead for its definition—a gift from God.

Because he was a peaceful baby with a cherubic face, warm brown eyes, and an impish grin, I gained a false sense of security as Matthew's gentleness paved the way for his more animated brother, Roman, to arrive. Roman entered the scene twenty-three months later and was something of a character from the outset, bearing a striking resemblance to his maternal grandfather with the personality to match. The qualities that served my dad so well as an entertainer and singer skipped right into Roman's soul, and he caught on early to the thrill of being the mastermind of antics. He would be the first child whose delight in his siblings' laughter outweighed his fear of getting into trouble. Roman interpreted a "no" to one of his little pranks as a sign that he hadn't refined it yet. This taught an otherwise trusting mother to stay on her toes. It would be Roman who would learn things like how to extricate himself from a baby seat, climb out of his crib headfirst with a tearless *thump*, and figure out the workings of the front door lock. The latter led to the subsequent horror of having a scantily clad two-year-old returned home after going door to door in our cul-de-sac looking for a snack—all while I went contentedly about my chores, thinking the children were taking their naps.

It would be Roman who would throw the forbidden ball in the house, shattering a priceless teacup, and then be reluctantly ratted out by his older siblings. Roman would be the child who, twenty-four hours after his daddy and another fireman replaced the linoleum in the bathroom and had the most expensive "uncloggable" toilet installed, would stuff a wide-toothed comb, two Hot Wheels cars, and his brother's electric toothbrush into it . . . proving that "uncloggable" means nothing when a determined toddler is around.

Had my senses been as heightened after the arrival of Matthew as they were after Roman, I might have been able to avoid an episode that was destined to haunt me for the rest of my life (and my husband for the rest of his career). If there are unspoken expectations for firefighters, I think it would be fair to say there are a few unspoken expectations for their wives as well. One is that we will not participate in situations that will bring undue attention to said fireman. No one had to tell me this, as this rule applied when I worked in the paramedic industry as well, but I wasn't a mother then. I had thought my previous paramedic experience would have made me a natural at the hard work of motherhood. Looking back, I can honestly say that my paramedic career did nothing to prepare me for this life.

The work had been exhausting, exhilarating, and oftentimes unpredictable. The stress of a shooting or serious auto accident could follow the relative comfort of a routine medical call. With enough experience I became confident of my skills and felt there was little that could intimidate me.

But it seems that the birth of each child required me to donate a substantial number of my brain cells, something they had failed to mention in Lamaze training, and which it took a dramatic incident for me myself to realize. The reality of my circumstances came to me one day after a lunch date with friends and my three then-small children (three, two, and six months). Precious little easygoing Matthew was the baby.

Merging onto the freeway after leaving the restaurant, Bailey, then only two, innocently asks, "Mommy, where's Matty?" "He's right here, honey," I responded, reaching behind me to stroke his soft cheek. *Nothing.* I reach around further, craning in my seat to look over my shoulder. *Nothing.* Oh my gosh, oh my gosh, the baby, where is the baby? Suddenly everything goes into slow motion. My brain freezes. Where am I? Where was I?. . . When was the last time I had the baby?

The sidewalk! I left the baby on the sidewalk! Oh, dear Lord. I realize with some horror I am several miles away from the next off ramp and can't just whip back to the restaurant. I grab my cell phone. "This is an emergency!" I shout at the unsuspecting waitress. "I just left my baby in his car seat in front of your restaurant four to five minutes ago; please get him; I'm on my way back right now." As I take the next off ramp and hurriedly wind my way through surface streets, stuck at every possible red light and behind the only hay truck for a hundred miles, I rack my brain to remember what happened. I had been saying goodbye to my friends. I'd set the baby down in the shade of the restaurant as I loaded his older brother and sister into the van. I'd walked around the back to make sure all the doors were closed and then driven away. Oh, help me!

Arriving at the intersection across from the restaurant, I see them: three police cars and a fire engine, emergency lights still flashing. Oh, this is not good, my husband is going to kill me. Fortunately for me, he isn't actually on duty today; he's across town playing softball with some of the other off-duty guys. He's probably listening to the sirens and thinking, "I'm glad I have the day off today." So am I, dear, trust me, so am I.

I fly into the parking lot, remnant pieces of hay sliding off the hood of my minivan. Frantic and embarrassed, I quickly approach an officer and explain who I am as the fire engines begin departing. "Don't leave me here alone, stay here and stand up for me," I want to plead. The thought quickly changes to, "Oh dear, I hope none of them recognized me."

Boy, do I feel foolish, sorry about you all having to come out here. Little oversight, you see, thought I could take my children out in public but my mistake, I'll take them back home and won't try this again. Peering at me over his sunglasses, lowered just enough to be intimidating, the seemingly high-school-aged officer says, "I'm sorry, ma'am, that won't be possible, could you please step over to the police car?" Won't be possible? What won't be possible? Who does this kid think he's talking to? I assure the officer that I am not crazy, I am a normal human who forgot my baby on a sidewalk. I am not an abusive mother.

Maybe I should tell him I'm married to one of the firemen, toss that whole professional courtesy trump card on the table and see if that helps. Or maybe I'll ask him if he knows the one about "What do firefighters and police officers have in common? They both want to be firefighters." Then I'll remind him how the fire department smoked their backsides in the annual fire/police softball game last year. Oh, yeah, I'm full of great ideas. On second thought, this might backfire, being that the officer thinks I'm a lunatic at this moment. Probably better I keep that card to myself lest my husband find out that I'm using his career to manipulate others. If I thought I had problems now, wait until I get home. The police/fire relationship can be tenuous and I don't want to upset the balance. Even in my desperate situation I want to protect my husband from the fallout of this, um, shall we say, minor incident.

But none of this makes any sense—why are they keeping the baby from me? I look across the parking lot at the officer holding my son, her arms cradling him to her chest as if to protect him from his crazy mother. "Please, let me hold my baby!" *No go.* "Take a deep breath," I remind myself; making a scene will only make the situation worse. I calmly ask to see the officer in charge. *Nope.* The adolescent in the uniform needs to ask some more questions, speaking slowly and purposefully as if I may be mentally impaired. I want to spank him for his disrespectful countenance, but I determine that this, too, will not help my case.

After the longest fifteen minutes of my life, spent answering questions and groveling pitifully, I ask to see the officer in charge again. The hall monitor who has been interviewing me says he will speak to him on my behalf. I shadow him as he saunters over to the commanding officer and I am given a moment to plead my case. With trademark suspicion the commanding officer listens to my pathetic little story. "When you called the restaurant to report what happened, how long did you tell them you had been gone?"

"Four to five minutes," I explain, breathless and desperate.

"Well, the waitress reported that you said, 'forty-five minutes.'"

Turns out the waitress who answered the phone, believing I was some kind of a lunatic, dialed 911 the moment I hung up, putting into motion the arrival of public safety personnel intent on protecting my recently "abandoned" baby, as if maybe I had left him for the taking and then had a change of heart four minutes later.

A bad phone connection almost cost my child a day in protective custody and me a tour of the local jail (from the inside)—not to mention the loss of my husband's faith in my mothering abilities.

My son was returned to the relative safety of my arms and I envisioned the scene that would greet Dan as the firefighters found out. And firefighters are just like elephants. They never forget. So much for my efforts to keep my husband's life outside the fire service uncomplicated.

It is four years before my husband's accident.

OUR KIDS KNOW THEIR ABCS

⁓

Okay, here's the problem. I've come to the painfully slow realization that Dan and I are not normal. No matter how much time I spend trying to convince myself otherwise, the fact still stands that compared to most of society, we're a little out there. Everything from the way we raise our kids to the way we spend our holidays indicates that we're on the fringe.

I've always told myself I'm this way because Dan and I have both worked in emergency medicine. With his job keeping me linked to the profession, I've never fully transitioned back to the preparamedic mindset. It affects the way I think, what I teach my children. It's in the way I can never sit and just relax at events where everyone else appears oblivious to the potential dangers lurking behind every corner. Family gatherings, BBQs, or even birthday parties can become a source of stress because I'm always looking ahead to what disaster may strike. Okay, there's a pool; keep a hawk eye on all the little ones, I'm somehow responsible for the safety of every kid in the place. BBQs have burn potential; I'm thinking of how to treat the wound before it happens. Beaches come with sand, sand ends up in eyes, I must have a fresh water supply ready to rinse them out quickly and so prevent blindness.

Oh, and a landing zone, I'm always thinking about a landing zone. Where can I have a helicopter set down in case one of the kids gets hurt in the jumphouse? Are there wires nearby, flight hazards? Where is the closest trauma center? Or is ground transport sufficient?

Laugh if you must, but being a former paramedic married to a fireman is a very stressful life. I am watching our children, I am watching your children, and I am prepared in case of emergency.

It never dawned on me how profoundly my past training and concerns could affect my life and the lives of the children until a friend of ours asked our son Matthew, five at the time, if he knew his ABCs. Matthew answered as cheerfully as any five-year-old would given an opportunity to display his newfound wisdom: "Airway, Breathing, Circulation."

I should have seen this coming. If I had spent just a little more time with normal people, I would realize the other parents actually jump up to assess the minor flesh wound of a skinned knee while the fireman and his wife sit still. We have learned the art of waiting to see if the child is really hurt or just surprised by the mishap. Sometimes you'll see the fireman squeeze the hand of the paramedic-turned-mother, reminding her not to react too quickly. My motherly instincts threaten to override my training.

Lest you think I have no heart, this is in no way to try and toughen our kids up or to be uncompassionate. It's merely an effort to triage the accident accurately without contributing to the problem with my emotions. I've learned the hard way that my response to the event is even more important than the event itself. An involuntary gasp is quickly followed by the calmness of, "Wow, nice fall, honey, good job catching yourself on your elbows like that, would you like a Popsicle?" The child, momentarily confused, reassesses the situation: *Well, my elbows are bleeding but my mom's not panicking so I must be okay.* Little does he know that Mommy is doing a head-to-toe survey and checking the dilation of his pupils for signs of a brain injury even as I ask, "Cherry or grape?"

The reality is that with more than twenty years of paramedic experience between us, there are very few things that we consider real emergencies. There are no such things as boo-boos and owies in our house. I sometimes joke that you've got to be bleeding from an artery or in flames to get Mom or Dad hustling out of their chairs.

Of course, if you really are injured you do get first-class treatment, but it's stern first-class treatment. The kids know better than to try to wriggle out of my arms if I tell them to sit still while I investigate a wound or ice a swollen forehead. I am transformed into Medic-Mommy as I remind the patient to lie still, breathe slowly, and keep his eyes on mine as I speak confidently, trying to reassure the child with a calm that deep down inside I no longer possess. This is, after all, not some stranger's child, but my own flesh and blood.

Which leads me to another point. The reason we have very few injuries in our home is that we are fully padded. There are covers on all the outlets, child safety locks on medicine chests and cabinets, and foam padding covering coffee table corners and fireplace hearths. There are spout covers for the tubs, rails for the beds, and devices for the toilet lids (to keep the babies from falling in and the toddlers from playing in them).

Then, of course, there are the rules, rules I'm assuming normal kids' parents don't have. Not because they don't care, but because they haven't seen the types of things I've seen, things that caused me to approach every call as a paramedic with the question, "How could this accident have been avoided?" I make a concerted effort not to let my children participate in activities with "trauma potential." This, of course, may send them all into therapy one day with stories of stifled childhoods, but I'll take my chances.

"Not so high on that swing, sweetie, you don't want to fall and get a cervical spine injury." "Slow down on your bike, bud, you don't want a compound fracture of your femur." "No, absolutely not, you may not play on the neighbor's trampoline. Have you any idea how many kids your daddy and I have seen hurt on trampolines? Open fractures of the radius and ulna, head injuries, and numerous strains and sprains. If God had wanted you to play on a trampoline He wouldn't have placed you in a home with two paramedics. You can bring the issue up with Him when you meet Him. Case closed." Only in our house will you hear the statement, "It's all fun and games until somebody gets a subdural hematoma."

Makes me sound pretty together, huh? The truth is, I didn't fare so well in the beginning of motherhood. When it came to my own kids I was anything but calm or objective. There is a serious downside to paramedic training, which is that it trained me to be an emergency hypochondriac. In a matter of moments I would have to be able to assess each call to its most critical potential. Without all the diagnostic equipment of a hospital or doctor, we assume that the injury is serious until proven otherwise. The doctor can work a diagnosis from the ground up, whereas paramedics go right to the top of the ladder (sudden death) and work our way down.

I proved that point when my daughter had one of her first mishaps. Now, before I launch into this story, I must remind the reader that I'd actually prayed for girls early into Dan's career. The thought was that girls are less risk-taking and thus would choose a career outside of the emergency medicine field. But I only have to look in the mirror to see that this isn't true in all cases. Then came my daughter. Suffice it to say that the bragging statement, "My sons have never been to an emergency room," is followed with the comment, "unless they're there to visit their sister."

Bailey has been a conundrum from the start. She is infinitely gentle and caring and incredibly tough. She'll be loving to a baby brother one minute, getting him a cup of juice or reading him a story, and the next moment I'll see her holding an older brother in a half-nelson trying to wrench a toy from him.

During the days of potty training I'd remind her every hour or so to use the bathroom to avoid the little accidents that happened to an easily distracted three-year-old. Always eager to please, she'd jump right up and run, not walk, to the potty. In this case her destination, the bathroom, would take her up one small step from the family room, through the dining room, and down a short hall. That's assuming we ever made it past the first step, which was a perfect location for a ballerina twirl, a twirl that one day resulted in a head plant into the corner of the wall.

Did I stay calm and apply direct pressure to the laceration, which appeared to run vertically from her hairline to the bridge of her nose? Yes. Did I keep it together, load the kids into the van, and get her to the doctor's office? Fat chance. I was on the phone calling 911 as fast as my fingers would dial. I was preparing a landing zone in my mind, as I was sure my child would need a neurosurgeon flown in for the open head wound that was so apparent. Recognizing both the paramedics on the ambulance, I rapidly gave them my assessment of the injury as well as my daughter's medical history. As the medics cleaned the wound I prepared to deliver my dissertation on wind direction and wire hazards for the helicopter.

Placing the Barbie Band-Aid cleanly across the tiny cut that revealed itself after wiping away the blood, the paramedic redirected my rescue efforts with a quick wink. "You can probably take her in for a couple of stitches later." As if to say, "Don't worry, we get it, it's different when you're a parent."

This experience prepared me somewhat for the times when Bailey knocked her front tooth out on a swing set and later dislocated her elbow at a park. The fact that I did contemplate a landing zone before packing her into the car and escorting her to the doctor's office reminded me that our family is still anything but normal.

SANTA IS A FIREMAN

Our holidays are a little out of the ordinary as well. While other families are gathering around Christmas trees loaded with heirloom ornaments, we could be celebrating at a fire station under a tree decorated with gauze bandages and tongue depressors, the children oblivious to the details of the décor as they wait for Santa to arrive on a fire engine. There is no delusion about Santa coming from the North Pole on a sleigh; at our house, Santa is a fireman. If questioned about this Santa/fireman thing my kids would be able to present their case like a miniature defense team.

Fact number one: Santa is a fireman because they see

the *same* Santa every year—not some imposter from the mall (insider information: it's Fireman Phil).

Fact number two: Santa is a fireman because he arrives promptly at Station One every year on the department's antique fire engine.

Fact number three: the only reason everybody else in the world doesn't know Santa is a fireman is because it's a secret only known by the firefighters' kids, a luxury allowed them because their daddies (and mommies, in some cases) work with him.

Fact number four: Santa has to be a fireman because he knows everything about every kid from the department who sits on his lap. He asks about their Little League teams, their pets, their brothers and sisters, and even some of their friends. He even knows in advance which kids' daddies will be on duty Christmas morning.

Fact number five: Santa wears a red suit because, as my soon-to-be-four-year-old will tell you, he needs to match the fire engine. He knows better than to go down the chimneys, as that would be too dangerous. The only thing this Santa goes down is a brass pole.

Fact number six: Santa always gives you something you really want, pulling it out of the big red bag he carries on the fire engine. It's never some cheesy plastic toy or a candy cane like other Santas give. It's as if this gift came right out from underneath the tree at home (which, of course, it did).

Fact number seven: Santa is a fireman because Santa is big, strong, and has a really deep voice, so his ho-ho-hos are really authentic. (Note: Fireman Phil is also a baritone singer.)

Fact number eight: Santa is a fireman because he knows how you feel inside, something only a fireman could understand. There's always a new kid at the station whose daddy just became a fireman. This kid doesn't want a gift, he just wants his daddy home for Christmas. Santa always knows just what to say. He tells the kid how proud he is to work with his daddy and what an important job his daddy does. Then Santa takes the new kid out and shows him his fire engine up close. He wipes away the child's tears so no one else will see him crying.

Of course Santa understands, because Santa is a fireman.

With all of this convincing evidence and Santa's popularity, it's no surprise when the kids barely notice the tones go off and their daddies rush off to a call. Santa, off shift for this event, will stay put until the family festivities are finished.

Tones going off are by no means an uncommon occurrence during family gatherings. All of the firemen's families coming to celebrate with their loved ones are aware of the risks—the risk that we will be eating without them.

The kitchens, filled with laughter and savory smells, are momentarily abandoned as the firemen rush out for a call and the wives rush in to complete the food preparation. We may finish the cooking, set the table, eat the meal, and clean up afterward, leaving enormous plates of food covered in plastic wrap for the men, before they ever return. It's far more the effort to be together, rather than actually *eating* together, that makes the holiday so special.

The kids, unaffected by the sudden disappearance of their fathers, are all too eager to wear themselves out climbing on the reserve apparatus (extra fire engines and the like), watching TV, coloring pictures, or drawing on the dry-erase boards. They are content to wait for their daddies' return for a kiss good night, leaving us moms hard pressed to drag the little ones home at a decent hour.

After a few of those experiences under the belt, some of the families resort to the alternative: rescheduling family gatherings around the firefighter's days off rather than the calendar. This has become an all-too-familiar routine in our family. As Dan's brother-in-law, Dave, is a fireman as well, trying to get together on an actual holiday can be an exercise in futility.

A phone call to Dan's sister, Eileen, is required to compare her husband's fire schedule with our fire schedule before we can plan the alternative family event. The day is chosen carefully in advance, our rescheduled holiday plans made, and Eileen still walks through the door husbandless. With a shrug of her shoulders and a resigned smile, she answers everyone's question with two words: "shift widow." Her husband has been called in for overtime.

OVERTIME

⁓

Overtime—the word that can instill dread in the heart of even the most hardened fireman's wife. True, not every firefighter finds himself in the position of taking overtime on a regular basis. Some firefighters aren't interested in it, some don't need the extra money. Some of the more seasoned firefighters have done their time and feel it's the younger generation's turn to pick up the slack. Others, their own children grown and gone, will gladly step in and work extra shifts regardless of their tenure.

But even seasoned firefighters can be stopped in their tracks by the addition of the word "mandatory." This single word establishes a clear delineation between the two types of overtime—the type the firefighter chooses and the type that chooses the firefighter. The first type of overtime can be a financial blessing to the family and might even be desirable. The second type can strike like lightning when those who are in charge of filling shift vacancies are forced to hold a firefighter at work to cover an immediate opening. The ball continues to roll downhill as the firefighter calls home with the news that all plans are off, as a twenty-four-hour shift becomes a forty-eight- or even a seventy-two-hour absence.

It's the unpredictability of the overtime that can be so frustrating. A department can be fully staffed, all shifts covered, and the next moment two or three men are injured in a fire. They go "off line," as they say, for days, weeks, or months, requiring every available firefighter to step up to the plate and help fill in the gaps.

I want to be supportive, really I do—but right when I think I'll be able to be encouraging and understanding of the overtime call, the fireman family phenomenon begins to occur. It is this phenomenon that makes the term *teamwork* feel like a noose around my reluctant throat, as my husband explains how he has a responsibility to the department and the other firefighters to help cover the shifts. These are the times when I want to remind him of his responsibilities at home. But in my heart I know he loves us and doesn't want to shirk his commitment to us, either; it's just that he can't be in two places at once. He trusts me to keep it together in his absence, and I am reminded how much he relies on me not to make his decision any more difficult than it is.

None of this information makes the phenomenon any more palatable. With the two things required for the phenomenon to begin already in place (Dan being held for extended duty and me being already tired), I must brace myself. At this moment, overtime has the appeal of a root canal or a pleasure cruise through the Bermuda Triangle. I hang up the phone and hear "ah-choo!" or the all-too-familiar *kathunk-whir, whir, whir, thump,* as a necessary appliance groans to its death. Whatever it is, it's destined to be out of service until Dan returns home three days later to repair it. Better yet, I can try to get a service technician over before Dan gets home. There is a tiny benefit to getting someone to come in to do repairs: it keeps Dan from coming home and spending his few days off tearing the thing apart and rebuilding it from the ground up. There's something about firefighters and their need to be able to fix everything and anything. If I call someone to fix it, I will invariably take a little grief for spending money for something "he could have done for free," but at least I'll be able to spend some time with my husband without having to pass him tools and listen to him mutter at an inanimate object. Or, he'll lament, if he couldn't fix it, one of the other guys could. It's well known that many of the firefighters come with talents from previous careers or may take advantage of their unique work schedules and have side jobs as carpenters, cooks, plumbers, landscapers, cement layers, window installers, business owners, etc.

The phenomenon continues with the assurance that if something is destined to go wrong, it will do so when Dan is gone. Vehicles will stop running, the electricity will go out, the plumbing will break, or all the toilets will become clogged. Or maybe the tree that has stood for thirty years unmoved by the gale-force winds of El Niño will come crashing through the roof during a gentle spring breeze. Someone will need stitches, the baby will need to see the doctor, the cat will need to see the vet, and I will be in need of a therapist. The otherwise healthy children will come down with the twenty-four-, forty-eight-, or seventy-two-hour flu, in direct correlation to the length of Daddy's shift. You wouldn't believe the illnesses that will come to an abrupt end one hour before Dan's return home, leaving him to wonder what Mommy's problem is.

The real downside to this dilemma, as if the aforementioned facts hadn't been enough, is my potential to become more delusional the longer Dan is away. Forgetting what struggle it took to get this job, I begin taking what Dan does for a living for granted. The admiration and respect I hold for the hard work he does begins sliding into the soup of my exhaustion.

Now, intellectually I am aware that my husband is at work. But emotionally it's an entirely different story. My little hormones begin attacking each other, undermining my ability to be rational. I imagine him and his little colleagues as co-conspirators in a hoax to be played on their unsuspecting families. If one of the wives phones, someone jumps on the overhead radio and pretends to tone out a call. In reality, he may be caring for sick people, helping victims of auto accidents, fighting fires, or training. Or maybe he's cleaning the station, maintaining the fire engine after a call, doing business inspections, or writing reports. But when I have been home for two or three days with a house full of kids who are throwing up every forty-two minutes and a broken washing machine, I don't care what he's doing, I just want him to come home.

Moreover, there's always the possibility that he's not on a call, that he's sitting around the firehouse in one of their custom recliners reading the paper, talking, watching the game, or playing dice, Ping-Pong, or pool, dining on the traditional fare of delicious firehouse meals, hot coffee, and, for dessert, fresh goodies baked by the loving hands of the grateful citizens of the community.

While Mommy, too tired to cook, serves Cheerios for breakfast, lunch, and dinner.

Maybe he's driving around in a clean red fire engine, waving at admiring children and the folks who appreciate everything he does. Notice that they take the fire engine everywhere, so as to always be the center of attention. They take it to the grocery store to do their shopping, smiling at the admiring public as they saunter up and down the aisles like a band of Chippendale's dancers. Once the show is over, they climb back into their fire engine, which, I might add, doesn't smell like old bananas and Happy Meals.

Then there are his nights of uninterrupted slumber, tucked cozily in his dorm, the rhythmic sound of soft snores lulling him to sleep. He can enjoy his hot morning showers without worrying that the other firemen are getting up before him to eat all the Oreos under the kitchen table or write on the wall with his new fuchsia lipstick.

Back at home, hours become days and I begin counting the minutes until he comes home, eager to pass him the baton of parenting. I relish the thought of thrusting a scantily clad baby into his arms on my way out the door. "Your turn!" I'll cheerfully announce as I bounce off to a day of child-free events. But when I see him drag himself across the threshold of our home with just enough energy left for the kids to crawl over him to say hello, I can't help but soften. My delusion melts away as my fireman hugs me, resting his head on my shoulder, and says gently, "It's good to be home," the weight of his absence suddenly outweighed by the relief of his return.

STRIKE TEAM

I SHOULD BE GRATEFUL that when he called to tell me about the overtime it didn't come with my two least favorite words, *strike team*.

As interesting, entertaining, and odd as life can be when you're married to a firefighter, there are some very real downsides to the experience. Firefighters and their families have to face uncommon risks and cope with difficult situations on an all-too-regular basis. One of the hardest parts for us is when Dan is called out for a strike team. Strike team—the same words that fill my heart with dread—fill his heart with longing. These are the opportunities for him to be deployed outside his district to support other departments in need. This means a chance to take his firefighting and rescue skills to places that are in the midst of a catastrophe or uncontrollable fire. He was given that chance when departments all over California and the nation were deployed to help with an enormous wildfire that had set thousands of acres ablaze in Southern California, destroying hundreds of homes and leaving dozens homeless, injured, or killed. The call for help from other departments, known as "mutual aid," requires firefighters to quickly prepare to take portions of their own teams on the road, leaving for several days, even weeks at a time, to assist in fighting the blaze.

There are moments when strike team duty is just too much for me. I have enough trouble understanding why he chooses to put himself at risk for a living. The idea of extending his efforts beyond his own town and community seems masochistic to me. But then I remember who he is. He's a fireman. The job is a part of him, not just something he does. His innate desire to help other people without constraint is part of why I love him.

The phone call came early in his shift. He was leaving for Los Angeles. I was ready to hustle the kids to the firehouse to say goodbye when he said, "I'm sorry, hon, but we're leaving now." I gathered the children and explained that Daddy was going out of town for a few days to help with the big fires in Los Angeles we'd been hearing about.

Our oldest son, Ben, burst unexpectedly into tears. "I don't want Daddy to die!" he sobbed. I drew him into my arms, comforting us both until his sobbing gave way to quivering breaths of resignation. Together we prayed for Daddy's safety. Dan had never been hurt, and the children had not been exposed to a line-of-duty death, but still they knew that Daddy's job was a dangerous one. The knowledge that he would be out of town brought with it an added insecurity that something bad could happen, and we wouldn't be close by to help.

The cold reality is that there are no boundaries in Dan's job. Although he may serve a particular area and be trained by that area's standards, when it comes to fighting fire, he'll go where the need is greatest. He is just one of the thousands of men and women who willingly cross city limits, borders, and sometimes cultures to become a united front.

This blaze alone would bring firefighters from all over the western United States and as far away as Japan. Different uniforms, equipment, training levels, and in some cases different languages, and yet they are one, brought together by the foe man has been fighting since the beginning of time. They do everything they can to bring its destruction to a halt before it can claim another acre, another home, another life. They try desperately to anticipate the fire's path of destruction, watching wind speed and direction to determine its destination, in an effort to limit risks to themselves and others. But sometimes, in spite of their training, best efforts, and calculations, things go wrong.

Partway down to the fires, Dan's caravan of engines and equipment was radioed to pull over for an update. Dan's former paramedic partner and friend from Oakland, Steve Rucker, had just lost his life in the blaze. Steve, a married father of two small children, was working for the Novato Fire Department at the time. Their strike team had gone down only a few days earlier. While trying to protect a home from the rapidly spreading fire, wind directions changed and the blaze turned on them unexpectedly. With the fire traveling at 30 mph, it was a miracle anyone survived. Rucker's captain, Doug McDonald, a man my husband had worked with in the past, had been critically injured as well. Dan called me on his cell phone from their temporary location to tell me the news.

I hung up the phone and cried. This one was too close to home. I cried for Steve's family, his widowed wife and fatherless children. I cried for Doug McDonald and his family; I could only imagine the strain they would face in the long months ahead with Doug's rehabilitation and recovery. I cried for the children and myself. The reality of the danger Dan was in slapped me full in the face. I cried for Dan. He had lost a friend and coworker, a loss he would not be able to mourn because of the job that lay ahead of him. He and the others would need to stay focused to fight the blaze that had taken their friend and colleague, their brother. And fight it they did. For three weeks, four hundred departments and more than three thousand firefighters came together to control the blaze. With the incredible amount of damage, it was a miracle that only one firefighter was lost. But one is too many. One is enough to remind us of the unpredictable life they lead, the risks that will be taken.

Dan's strike team returned five days later, after a sudden change of weather gave the firefighters the upper hand in the fight. Although they were tired, hungry, and spent, there was still the unfinished business of putting their fallen brother to rest.

The children and I stood on a freeway overpass watching miles of fire engines, ambulances, and police cars usher Steve's body back to his waiting family and colleagues. Clinging to the chain-link fence of the overpass, we tried to display our love and respect to those who passed beneath us. Our sign read GOD BLESS THE FIREFIGHTERS, REST IN PEACE STEVE RUCKER.

Five thousand firefighters arrived in Marin, California, for Steve's funeral. Fire engines came from as far away as New York to show their support. The parking lot of the Marin Civic Center looked like a sea of silver and red, as brightly polished engines sat patiently in solemn assembly. In the midst of them another tribute to Steve could be seen on the engines from L.A.: freshly painted inscriptions on their doors reading IN MEMORY OF STEVE RUCKER.

Firefighters and their families are always aware that they may be forced to lay down their hopes and dreams for the career. Whether the firefighter is working in his or her own town or as part of a strike team, the risks are always present.

THE GOOD, THE BAD, AND THE UGLY

BEING RELATED TO SOMEONE in the fire industry means I can't outrun the risks of my loved one's career choice, but the dangers are sometimes easier to tolerate in light of the unique benefits. When the firefighting calendar isn't inundated with overtime, the schedule can be amazingly free, allowing us to spend significant amounts of time together as a family. The profession is interesting and exciting, and I definitely enjoy hearing firsthand about some of the wonderful calls Dan runs.

The most interesting runs are the "saves." On these calls, had the firefighters or paramedics not arrived in the nick of time, not had the right tools or training, the patient wouldn't have survived.

In the wee hours of an October morning, a call came in for a woman down. "Unconscious and unresponsive" were the only details known, as the engine and ambulance roared to the call for help. On scene, firefighters were met with a hysterical woman in her twenties. "Inside, she's inside!" the distraught daughter shouted as she rushed them into the living room of her parents' modest home. The firefighter/paramedics on the ambulance came in directly behind the engine crew and found themselves momentarily confused. The few hours of sleep they'd gotten prior to this emergency meant that everyone was a little foggy. Dan and his partner quickly glanced around the room and saw only what appeared to be an older man kneeling before a chair praying. Mystified, Dan turned to his captain, Rick King, and asked, "Where's our patient?"

"Right there," the captain gestured, pointing to the legs of the man who knelt several feet ahead of them.

It was then that they saw the woman. Her husband, who was trying desperately to provide mouth-to-mouth resuscitation to his wife, was straddling the unconscious patient.

Initially reluctant to turn over his lifesaving efforts, the husband was coaxed into providing the firefighters with the details of this crisis and giving the paramedics the access they needed to his wife.

Blue from the chest up, her body lay lifeless, her eyes staring vacantly beyond those before her as she made her last dying attempts to breathe. One, two, three breaths a minute was all the fight she had left as an unexpected asthma attack prepared to mortally separate her from her husband and child.

The firefighters and paramedics went to work. Their firefighting roles quickly transferred into positions of medical care. George Vedder, Dan's partner for the shift, took his role seriously, and quickly began pulling out the medications and supplies Dan would need. The engineer, Fred Clement, began the task of bringing in the gurney and preparing the patient for transport. The engine's third man, Juancarlos Colorado, a former paramedic, worked as Dan's extra set of hands, expertly assisting the patient's airway one minute and helping to prepare the patient for an IV the next. A breathing tube was placed in the patient's throat as her heart rate soared from 120 beats a minute to an ominous 180, indicating a heart starving for oxygen. The firefighters and paramedics worked feverishly to keep her heart beating as they struggled to force oxygen into her spasmed lungs and administer lifesaving medications. She was transferred to the ambulance as the paramedics worked frantically to keep her alive. Moments before arriving at the hospital, the patient began to take her first breaths.

The grateful family waited outside the emergency room to thank the firefighters and paramedics for their quick response, which saved the life of their beloved wife and mother.

There was the man who survived against all odds after being extricated from a demolished vehicle. The young mother brought back to life after suffering an unexpected heart attack. The healthy baby delivered a few minutes earlier than expected, much to the chagrin of its parents, in a convenience store parking lot. These are the calls that my husband lives for. They're the reason he got into the job in the first place: to make a difference in someone's life.

Communities are beginning to recognize some of these almost miraculous events with ceremonies referred to as survivor reunions. It's a gathering of all those who were involved in a dramatic rescue, where they get to meet their patient face-to-face after recovery. These are truly incredible moments not only for those whose lives were touched by the rescuers, but for the rescuers themselves. All too often the firefighters and paramedics see the patient only during the most difficult part of the event; they rarely get to see the successful outcome of their efforts. These ceremonies provide closure for the patients, who sometimes have limited recollections of the event, and also provide much-appreciated encouragement to the folks who don't always get to hear the heartfelt words that the patients may long to say.

In spite of the frustration I often feel, I know from watching these ceremonies that the chance to save a life makes all the bad stuff worthwhile, because the bad stuff seems to come more often than the good. The calls that leave the rescuers crestfallen to discover that they couldn't save a life. The call that leaves no outward sign of damage but will invariably leave its mark on the inside of each firefighter involved.

There are those times, too, when I realize the second he walks through the door that something is wrong. It can be in the subtle way he answers me when I ask how his shift was. A normal response of "good," "quiet," or "busy" is replaced with "Last night was a rough one." Those statements make me stop what I'm doing and prepare myself to listen.

I've watched the metamorphosis take place as Dan unconsciously begins to compartmentalize his life, determining to keep his work experiences and home life separate. The interesting discussions of shift details slowly give way to only the highlights he feels comfortable sharing. Many times I realize that he eliminates some of the painful events of his shift to protect me. He doesn't want to tell me anything that would cause me to worry more about him. I appreciate his efforts, but it hurts my heart to see him erect a wall of self-protection around himself as he evolves into a seasoned firefighter, taking with it the idealism and innocence he once possessed.

It seems reasonable that home would be the place where he would safely retreat from the memories of a bad call, a place to separate himself from the people, sights, sounds, and smells that remind him of tragedy. But some of these calls follow him home, clinging to him like the smell of smoke in his bunkers, the burden too personal to leave behind.

This would be one of those times. Dan sat with me on the sofa and told me about a terrible call they'd had the night before where a small child lost her life. The firemen and paramedics used all of their skills and equipment to reverse the damage a car accident had caused to her fragile body, but the extent of her injuries was incompatible with life. He needed to talk, to review the details of the event, in an effort to remind himself that everything possible had been done. The only thing I could do at this point was to let him recall the story and work through the feelings. Time and talking are sometimes the only sources of comfort I can offer.

I tried not to give advice or try to fix it for him; instead I just listened and waited for him to come to a place of acceptance. I knew this call, like so many others, would be stored in the files of his memory, and would occasionally open while he slept or flash before him at unexpected times. The stories are processed and stored but never forgotten.

It can be hard to accept that repressing such painful experiences can actually be instrumental to his ability to function. Tragic calls can and do come on the heels of one another, leaving no downtime in between. Time to stop and process his feelings after a crisis is a luxury he is not afforded. The very next patient has the unspoken expectation that his or her emergency will be on the forefront of his mind, completely oblivious to events that may have immediately preceded their emergency.

It's the hidden stresses that concern me. The calls, some of which would horrify most of society, seem run-of-the-mill to him. I fear these calls have the intrepid ability to eat away at his emotional well-being, one piece at a time. The process is so slow and silent that he's not even aware of the changes I see taking place in him. The good calls remind me how much I love the fire service for what it's brought into his life. But the bad calls remind me how much I hate it for what it's taking out.

It's even harder to realize that there's nothing I can do to repair it for him. I can listen, I can watch, I can wait for the time when he's willing to open up, but I cannot force him.

Dan stood up wordlessly and headed for the garage to find some distraction. He couldn't talk about the call anymore; it was just too close to home. I gave him his distance for a few minutes and then stepped out after him to see if there was anything I could do to help. He stood before a half-loaded washing machine, one of our two-year-old's jumpers held lovingly in his hands, tears streaming silently down his cheeks. I slipped my arm around his waist and just waited as he fought this battle alone for a moment. He stood temporarily entranced as water lapped over soiled articles of clothing and slowly set the jumper into the embrace of warm, sudsy water. The machine thunked into its agitation cycle, and the trance was broken. Dan swept the tears away with the quick brush of each arm, closed the lid, and gave me a kiss on the cheek. "I'm okay," he reassured me, stepping back into his personal armor, and the moment was gone. He would not be able to talk about this event again; it had been stored away with the others. I, on the other hand, would need to take these feelings to someone who understood: the wives.

PART OF THE PACKAGE

Before becoming firefighters, the people preparing for this profession know what they're getting into. Most of them have spent weeks, months, or years around the fire service before joining up. The families are not so fortunate. Their training doesn't begin until the firefighter returns home from the first shift on duty. Over time they may witness subtle or even major changes in their loved one's personality, without having the first clue as to what's happening or how to help.

Although there are constant improvements in the development of support systems for families, sometimes nothing is more helpful than the support of the other firemen and their wives. More than once I had turned to the listening ears of a wife who could do nothing more than say she understood. The fact that she knew what I was going through was enough to keep me from feeling alone with my concerns.

Many of the more seasoned wives will take the younger ones into the fold much like the older firemen do with the new recruits. Some departments even have wives' groups and auxiliaries that meet on a regular basis. They get together for fundraisers and charitable events, have a few laughs, talk about their husbands' similarities, and grumble a tiny bit about the impact the job has had on their families. The wives become as connected as the firemen in some cases. They help encourage and support each other over the hurdles that inevitably arise in all of their lives. This connection was never displayed more vividly to me than when one of the wives in a neighboring department was diagnosed with breast cancer. The other firemen's wives were with her every step of the way. They cooked meals, cleaned for her, and took care of every conceivable issue that could arise. Their husbands held up their end by donating hours to her husband's sick fund and covering his shifts every time she had an appointment for chemotherapy or radiation so he could be by her side. The loyalty shared by the brothers in blue knows no boundaries when it comes to their families as well. Their time, talents, vacations, savings accounts, and personal belongings are quickly offered up to another in need.

There are also veteran wives who come with a life full of experience and advice free for the taking. Every department has its own version of Alice Gloeckner, a wife in Dan's department. Alice, in spite of her well-earned air of confidence, possesses a heart of compassion and understanding that comes only from being married to a firefighter-turned-captain-turned-battalion-chief with thirty years of experience, not to mention the added bonus of having three sons, all of them firemen as well.

Reaching out to someone as experienced and grounded as Alice can be a wealth of support for those who wonder if they will ever survive as wives in this profession. A veteran wife can remind the new wives not to take it personally when the firemen are temporarily withdrawn after a difficult shift. She offers them coping techniques, like allowing the men to have a reentry period when they first return home before giving them an agenda or list of projects to tackle. When a wife is concerned about a sudden change in her husband's behavior—if he appears to be struggling with the side effects of a particularly difficult call—no one can relate better than the wife of another fireman. Even with outside resources available for help as departments offer confidential employee counseling and addiction services, some fire families will prefer to keep the issues in-house, which means that a wife may go to another wife who will mention something to her husband who may in turn pull his brother aside and offer some support. Sometimes the men open up to, and receive feedback from, a colleague better than anyone else. There is very little that goes on in the lives of firefighters that one of them hasn't been through before.

It became apparent early on that being married to a firefighter wasn't going to be observation, but much more audience participation. I became a part of the job, the struggles, the support, and the concerns of his profession the day Dan became a fireman.

GREATER LOVE . . .

NEVER WOULD THE LEGACY of our connection to each other be driven home more than on September 11, 2001. For the families of firefighters throughout the world, it wasn't just the horror of what took place on our homeland or the grief that consumed us. For the families of firefighters, the attack was personal. We imagined the faces of our own loved ones in every lost uniform. The names and faces of the lost men were unfamiliar, but their hearts were filled with the same loyalty, sacrifice, and commitment to others that we knew. We were related to each other as we waited, watched, and prayed with every firefighter's family in the world that just one more firefighter would be found alive.

All of America saw past the frailties and weaknesses often associated with public servants that day, and saw the sacrifice given by those who don a uniform of any color to signify their commitment to the safety of our country and its people.

The New York City Fire Department was not alone in this disaster. Its inherent connection to every firefighter in the world just became more apparent. Firefighters and their families were suddenly all involved in some sort of effort to help those who had been left behind. Fundraisers, blood drives, and support programs for the hundreds of widows and children of the fallen heroes were in full swing in every department. Still other firefighters left their own families, friends, and homes behind to board planes, load belongings into vehicles, and head for Ground Zero to dig through the rubble.

The people and communities unrelated to the fire service showed their compassion and respect for the loss as they showered their support and sympathy on neighborhood fire stations with food, flowers, and cards of encouragement that continued to come in for weeks.

People everywhere seemed to realize that every firefighter in the world ran that last call, imagined the pressure, considered the risks, climbed the stairs in their minds. They were helping the scared, the confused, and the lost to find their way home, rushing past them, stopping only to render aid or offer breaths of fresh air from their own masks, to reach those who were higher up. They were going in and up while everyone else was going down and out. Each one was wondering, would they have heard the rumbling? Would they have realized what was happening in the end?

And the brothers and sisters, bound invisibly to one another, cried, some behind closed doors, some openly, some in the arms of their families, and some silently. But they all mourned, they all shared in the loss. We cried with them as we saw the list of names on the department's dry-erase and chalkboards grow longer every day, until every man was accounted for, 343 of them. We mourned in our hearts with their families as the symbol of each man was buried, putting to rest a life well lived.

The lost men are still honored in my husband's department today, as I'm sure they are in a myriad of departments throughout the world. An enormous collage with the pictures and names of all those who gave their lives sits center stage on the wall of the main station's day room, keeping the memories and legacy of every man alive.

The healing has begun. As time continues her journey forward and the fire service transitions back into life as they know it, the loss of these colleagues remains firmly tucked in their hearts: Steve Rucker, from the strike team in Southern California; the New York firefighters; the thousands of other men and women who risk their lives daily.

They remain nameless to those who didn't know them personally, but have given the ultimate sacrifice. These men and women give meaning to the words found in John 15:13: "Greater love has no one than this, that he lay down his life for his friends."

HERO AT HOME

HERO. THE WORD WAS heard a lot after September 11. Dan and most of the firemen he worked with are not comfortable with the title. They feel that it's a word that should be reserved for folks who risk their lives unexpectedly, not those who choose danger as part of their job description. This in no way takes away from some of the heroic things firefighters do, but acknowledges that they do what they do for the love of the job. Risking their lives on occasion comes with the territory. Lifesaving is something they train for and anticipate while carefully measuring the cost to themselves and others. The risks are calculated, but not taken lightly.

They have a saying in the fire service that goes something like, "A firefighter will risk a lot to save a life, a little to save property, and even less to save lives and property that are already lost."

It serves no purpose for firefighters to risk their lives unless they truly believe they may save a life in the process. A firefighter dying in the line of duty to save a house is not a victory.

Do I think of Dan as a hero? Well, yes, of course he's a hero of sorts to me. I admire the sacrifices he makes to train and work for the benefit of others. I am comforted by his commitment to me and the children, and by his integrity. These are the things that make him a hero in my eyes.

But there are others who see him as a hero the moment he walks through the door, regardless of what he says, people who are oblivious to his training, his work ethic, and his desire to do everything he can for them. They are not just impressed with the uniform and the badge. They love and admire their hero simply because he's their dad.

Don't believe for a second that Dan's job as a firefighter is lost on our kids. Au contraire. They love going to visit him at the firehouse, and the older ones always ask about the types of calls he runs. They are very excited about what he does for a living, but his hero status comes simply because of the way they look up to him and look forward to seeing him, and the way he makes them feel special.

This is never more apparent than when he comes home

from an extended shift. He'll try to sneak through the front door, stealthily give me a kiss, set his work bag down, and assume his receiving position before being spied by the first little one. He is just waiting to be spotted, quietly setting himself on the floor like a venus flytrap anticipating its first victim.

"Daaaadyyy!" The reveille brings the tallest to the smallest racing into the room. The children bounce with anticipation as they wait the few seconds for their turn to run into his arms, outspread to catch them. Throwing himself back onto the floor with great exaggeration, Dan then bounces back up like a giant Weeble, allowing the children to feel as if they are truly strong enough to knock him over. The ritual does not end until the smallest set of footie pajamas has padded its way into Daddy's arms with peals of delight. The only thing that can top these festivities is Daddy jumping up to pull a pink cardboard box adorned with ordinary string from his work bag: "Doooonuuuts!"

This ritual is only one of the reasons Dan's days off change the entire mood of the household. He's instantly at the top of the "good guy/hero" list in the eyes of the kids. His presence instantaneously turns the home I struggled to maintain while alone into a circus. With chores forgotten and routines interrupted, the children vie for their dad's attention, eager to tell him about their most recent accomplishments and discoveries.

I have to will away the vision I have of myself as a warden, comforting myself with the knowledge that I am trying to run two entirely different households on a revolving basis. For reasons of personal sanity, I try to maintain order and keep some semblance of a schedule for a single mom with five kids when Dan is gone. There are many days I'm just glad I can tell him his kids are alive. But all bets are off the moment he returns home.

Our day's schedule always depends on how long he's been gone, how much he's slept, and whether he comes home with a secret mission in mind. These missions have been known to send all of Mommy's plans flying out the window. We might be going to visit one of the other firemen, who lives on a dairy farm where we can feed the baby cows; or maybe we'll pack the family up and go the beach for the day to study the tide pools.

Of course there are always the days when he comes home with only one possible option available to him—sleeping after an exhausting shift. This in no way alters the children's perspective of him; they're just glad he's home. They're content to quietly loiter around the locked bedroom door, waiting for him to wake like a bunch of groupies hoping for a chance to see their favorite rock star.

I tell myself he can maintain his status as the good guy, just like the grandparents can, because he isn't bogged down with the daily workings of the household. He can focus his energy on listening to animated stories, playing, wrestling, and being a constant source of entertainment. Shopping, laundry, housecleaning, and meal-making are Mommy's domain. I'm in more of an indentured servant position. I'm viewed as a chauffeur, cook, and maid—not exactly a rock star. I'm hardly the kind of person the kids jump up and down in anticipation of seeing; I'm more like the person who gets them a drink while they wait for the real superstar to show up.

I also have the occasionally unpleasant task of having to be the boss when Daddy's gone. When you're a fireman's wife, the telltale line, "Wait till your father gets home!" just doesn't work. I have trouble remembering what I had for breakfast; I'd have to keep a journal to remember what transgressions took place during his absence. To keep the peace, I have to be willing to deal with issues on the spot. My best efforts to be both judge and jury unravel with the simple question, "When is Daddy coming home?"

NEAT IDEA

As MUCH FUN as it was to have our own hero at home, I realized that I was still pushing the painful memories of September 11 around like so many vegetables on my plate. I kept thinking they would somehow go away with the passing of time or the constant massaging of the details. But it was a struggle to separate myself from the events, as I felt inexplicably woven to the families of those lost firefighters. For a short time the world stood still as the reports of firefighters discovered in the rubble diminished. Then came the reports about other firefighters being lost in different fires and rescues that went awry. The heightened sense of insecurity seemed to loom like a swollen cloud over all of us.

Finally, our hearts began to heal with the passing of time, and it came with the news that we were expecting another child. Now, crazy as five kids sounds to some, we were elated to have another new blessing preparing to enter our home. I eagerly anticipated the relief from sorrow that tragedy had brought, and basked in the joy and challenges the pregnancy and expectation of new life would bring for us.

More than ever, I was grateful that Dan was safe in the confines of our small town, the Chicken Capital of the World. I was completely content to watch the household hero wrestle with the kids on his mornings home. We were on our way back to normal, and everything was going to be okay.

Let the nesting begin! Now, if that's not a weird phenomenon, I don't know what is. I was no longer content to sweep, vacuum, mop, and dust. No, now I had to wash out all the cabinets and drawers in the house with bleach and water before returning their unsterile contents to the make-believe sterile environment. I was determined to scour corners, nooks, and crannies that hadn't been touched since the last baby arrived.

There were rooms that suddenly needed fresh dressings of paint, window edges that had to be cleaned with Q-tips, and all sorts of new and exciting projects for Dan to do. There were even some old projects I didn't realize he'd gotten so far behind on. If I could just get him home from the firehouse to join in the fun of nesting! But right about the time my nesting began, the department had a sudden onslaught of overtime availabilities, and Dan missed out on all these projects I had for him, poor guy.

I had plenty of things to keep me occupied those last few weeks. Dan justified the overtime by reminding me that we had to pay for all the paint and cleaning supplies.

I found some new designs for my nesting instincts this go-round, and made some more safety advances for our home. There were updated emergency boxes in the cars with flares, water, Band-Aids, aspirin, blankets, snacks, and anything else I could squeeze in, as well as an emergency contact book for the home in case something were to go wrong when a babysitter was in attendance. Lord forbid Roman should pull one of his little pranks on an unsuspecting child-care provider, and they were to find themselves unaware of how to get help or give directions to our home in a crisis. Names and numbers of doctors, neighbors, and relatives would be needed, and now could be found in the little book that sits under the phone on the file cabinet adjacent to my desk.

The pregnancy seemed to waddle toward its enlarging conclusion in record time. Dan couldn't get enough overtime to keep from being roped into wallpapering and painting everything I could think of. Roman and the new baby would be sharing a room blanketed in brilliant blue for the top half and fire-engine red on the bottom, with a tiny border of trains running around the wall at waist level. Ben and Matty had been moved into the guest room, whose fire-engine theme was now replaced by a space motif. Daddy had even given Bailey's room a face-lift, the utilitarian white walls giving way to sunny yellow and cotton candy pink. The kids, excited that their rooms had all been updated as part of the preparations for the new baby, were more eager than ever to meet the newest member of the family. All that was left was to watch the clock and wait and wait and wait.

I did everything I could think of to keep the kids occupied during the last few weeks of my pregnancy. While Dan was away during a greatly unappreciated heat wave in the middle of August, I rotated from a padded deck chair— where I could watch the children dance in the wading pool and careen in the slip-n-slide—to beaching myself like a sea cow on our new (praise the Lord) spring-filled sectional sofa. I was large, it was hot, but we were happy.

Lisa Schweizer, now there is one woman who understands my dilemma. We spent many an afternoon on the phone complaining about the heat, late stages of pregnancy, and that irritating overtime. If I thought my love of unscheduled overtime had been minimal in the past, it was nothing compared to my current level of distaste. Lisa understood. It helped a whole lot that she had two small children, one of them a colicky newborn. And where was her husband? Away doing overtime with my husband, of course. Relieved, I'm sure, both of them: one to have a break from a colicky baby, and the other to have a break from a colicky wife. Oh, those lucky boys.

"Lisa, I could write a book about this. We can't be the only two women in the world who have to deal with these issues from the fire service."

"Yep," she agreed, I should write a book. With all the free time I was about to have on my hands, homeschooling three of my four small children and toting a newborn baby on my hip, all while married to a man who was home less than half the time. It was a wonderful idea.

We laughed and hung up the phone, and I sat, mostly because sitting was about the easiest thing one could do in my condition. The kids were still playing contentedly in the garage in an effort to avoid the midday heat, so I took advantage of the opportunity and grabbed the notepad from the end table next to me and began to scribble notes. At the top of the page, in blunt pencil, came the only title possible, *The Fireman's Wife*. Now we were on to something. I jotted down an outline that I hoped every fireman's wife would understand: the overtime, the worry, the exhaustion, and the pride. Surely we wives must have these things in common. Then my brain kicked in, and I began to rethink my position.

Who was I to write about being married to a fireman? I hadn't had any real experience with worry or fear, not like those precious families in New York. What on earth did I have to offer to people who knew nothing of my family or me? I came without credentials, had no writing experience and certainly no life experience that would be of interest to others. I'd had my share of loss in life and my share of struggles, too, but very few related to Dan's job. It was a neat idea, but I didn't think I was the one for the job. I stuffed the notepad on the bottom of a bookshelf and put the idea to rest. In only a few days a new baby would arrive, taking with it any illusion I had of free time to write a book.

It is eleven weeks before my husband's accident.

AND THEN THERE WERE FIVE

I T ' S A B O Y! Another robust baby boy, named Michael this time, after my extremely funny and constantly supportive brother. The children hover over the newest member of the family, touching his chubby arms and legs, delighting in the reflexive grasp of his tiny fingers that wrap around their own.

Ben and Matty want to know when he'll start talking and walking so they can play catch with him. Bailey never wants him to grow up, and Roman is far more in love with the new baby than we could have imagined. (Because he will have an apprentice to train, no doubt.) We have been in no small way blessed with a baby with a peaceful countenance, perfectly agreeable to being jostled and held by a team of admirers. Everyone's eager for their chance to hold him, wrap him in a blanket, stuff a binky (our pacifier nickname) into his rosebud mouth, or rock him in Mommy's rocking chair. The fan club only becomes scarce when there's a diaper to be changed.

Four weeks later I am kneeling for bedtime prayers next to Ben and Matty's beds, paralyzed with fear.

This has been happening off and on since Dan returned to work from his paternity leave two weeks ago. It's always the same feeling—a sense of impending doom, that Dan's in danger. I've told Dan every time it's happened. Our lengthy discussions reveal that my immediate concerns have been unwarranted, and we address the probability of it being hormone-related. He reminds me gently that he can't go to work worrying about what might happen. He does his best to be safe and conscientious, and I need to trust that he will do everything possible to come home again.

I am reminded of my favorite punch line of all time: "Get in the wheelbarrow!" I love telling that joke, and it seems to be especially relevant right now. It's the one about the tightrope walker who is creating excitement and tension with the audience several hundred feet below him. He's got a wheelbarrow positioned before him on the tiniest of ropes, and he stands precariously close to the edge of his platform, beckoning to the excited faces below. "Do you believe I can cross this tightrope, no safety net in place, without falling?" Sure of his reputation as an experienced tightrope walker, the eager audience yells back in support, "We believe you can do it!"

"Do you really trust me?" he yells, building the wave of anticipation.

"We trust you," the crowd screams back in unison. The tightrope walker signals for his assistant to point to one of the most zealous members of the audience and says, "Then get in the wheelbarrow."

That's faith: putting action into the very thing you say you believe in. In my case, I'm just going to have surrender my whole fear issue to God. It's cheaper than being medicated, and He's the only one who can affect the outcome. Dan's tired of hearing about my fear, I'm tired of talking about it, and God's probably tired of me meddling with it. So I'm just going to have to let it go.

Ahhhh! The cool weather is arriving, as November begins her descent toward December and the baby and I are finally getting some much-needed rest. We're working on a routine of being awake in the daytime and sleeping a little at night, putting teeth in the statement that says, "The bridge between hope and despair is often a good night's sleep." No one can appreciate that statement more than a mother who hasn't slept in six weeks. At ten weeks old, Michael's getting the hang of sleeping at night, and Mommy couldn't be happier.

Overtime has fallen off a little, and Dan's schedule has allowed him to go back to taking off his regular four days for a change. I am relieved to be spending a family morning together with nothing but a free day ahead of us. The kids are clamoring over each other for a place to sit on the sofa, as the baby and I take refuge in a nearby chair as we prepare for our family devotions, when Dan's cell phone begins to ring. He jumps up quickly, plucking it off the kitchen table, hoping to minimize the interruption for the sake of the kids' limited attention spans.

"Hello? . . . Hey, Captain . . . sure . . . yes, sir . . . I'll be right in."

He doesn't need to say a word. I know this drill, it's the overtime again.

"Hey, guys, I've gotta go," he says, getting the attention of the kids. He turns to me. "They've got a big fire going down on Kentucky Street, and everybody's being called in." I don't like the interruptions any more today than I did when this began seven and a half years ago, but I understand. "Okay, everybody, give Daddy a kiss goodbye."

"Awwww, Dad," comes the disappointed response.

"I'll be back shortly, you guys," he says with a knowing wink. He grabs his jacket from behind the front door and gives us all a quick peck, tousling the hair of the boys.

"I love you, honey, be safe, you're my best friend." My words safely in place, he walks out the door.

"Ditto."

It is two hours before my husband's accident.

REPORTING FOR DUTY

TEN MINUTES AWAY from home, Dan crested the hill leading into Petaluma and saw the blanket of black smoke rising on the west side of town. His heart raced. A big fire in historic downtown was something they always anticipated and trained for. He just hoped he was in early enough to be on the front line. The earliest firemen into the stations would get suited up, climb on the reserve engines, and head for the fire. Those who arrived later would man the stations for backup support and run medical aids or other emergency calls for help. Getting there in time to be assigned to an engine and sent to the fire was a coveted position.

Dan pulled into headquarters and saw several extra

cars in the station's parking lot. He jumped out of his car, entered through the back doors of the station, and let the captain know he was ready to go to work. Unfortunately, because he was the only paramedic to have arrived thus far, he was told he'd be assigned to an ambulance. His heart sank. He had really hoped to be at the fire.

Sean McCarthy, one of the probationary firefighters, entered the day room and approached Dan with trademark probie eagerness. "Are we here in time to get an engine?"

"No," Dan replied, "looks like you're stuck with me on the ambulance, Big Mac. Sorry about that."

"No worries, man, at least we're working together," Sean said with a smile.

Before Sean and Dan had a moment to resign themselves to their assignment or pour themselves a cup of coffee, Captain Epperson approached. "We need you guys to mount up and head for the fire, they're calling in reinforcements."

"Awesome!" was Sean's elated response. "Let's go!"

Dan and Sean were in the ambulance and headed for the fire in a flash.

They parked less than a block away, grabbed their equipment, and headed for the command post to receive an assignment. Chief Ahlin directed them to take care of utilities (which in firespeak means to turn off all gas and electricity to the involved buildings). They quickly headed to the alley behind the blazing building, while Sean silently lamented about the bummer assignment. He really wanted to be fighting fire. Their assignment completed, they picked their way through the back alley, stepping over hoses and around the enormous engines, and headed for the command center to await another assignment. Rounding the corner of the building, Dan and Sean both heard shouting and looked up in unison to see a captain summoning to them from the roof requesting their assistance. The directive was to grab chain saws and head for the adjacent buildings to trench-cut the roof and halt the fire's progress. They quickly reported to the battalion chief and headed for their new assignment.

Equipment in hand, they headed up the ladder. Dan eased himself onto the roof and began to assess the situation through the haze of smoke. He nodded to his captain as he and Sean positioned themselves on opposite sides of the building's peak and brought their chain saws to life.

WHERE THERE'S SMOKE, THERE'S FIRE

MIKE ORTELLE STOOD OUTSIDE his modest Petaluma home on the west side of the freeway and scanned the morning's crisp autumn sky. He loved this town, had spent his whole life here, had met and married Liz, his wife of more than twenty years, here. The two of them were perfectly content to raise their seven children in this town as well.

It was with a little pang of disappointment that he had never gotten hired by the local fire department, but an offer had come from a department thirty miles south before Petaluma had an opening, and his career had taken root there.

Fifteen years on the job, and he could smell trouble before he saw it. Something was out of place. Just west of where he stood he could see a small black plume rising directly above the downtown area. The smoke was dense and dark, which told him there was no water on it, as water on fire quickly dilutes smoke to shades of gray. More ominously, there were, as of this moment, no sirens to be heard. To Mike, this meant the fire had, as of yet, gone unreported.

He hurriedly passed the extra gallon of milk he'd been retrieving from the garage to the waiting hands of his daughter and yelled to Liz, "Honey, there's a fire downtown, I'll be back." Liz was all too familiar with this abrupt change in their morning. The adage that "where there's smoke, there's fire" is never a complete statement until you add, "and every firefighter in a ten-mile radius." Off duty or on, firefighters go to watch, to learn, and to help. Mike was going to do all three.

The short drive to the downtown area brought Mike in alongside the first arriving engines. He jumped out of his car and made his way across the street to watch and wait as local and mutual-aid firefighters began breaking into divisions. Groups of firefighters were being set apart for an interior attack, apparatus assignments, and exterior assignments. Mike was familiar with the protocol. Positions would be broken into two categories, offensive (those who would attack the fire) and defensive (those who would work to prevent the fire from spreading). The departments would have to work quickly to fight what was already an aggressive blaze.

He moved with familiarity along storefronts until he found what he was looking for. He entered the building and made his way up a side entrance leading to a rooftop for a better view. Store employees and local business owners hurriedly began making their way to similar positions along the tops of businesses to gain the best vantage points to watch the firefighters contain the rapidly spreading fire.

It was frustrating to listen to some of the questions and comments made by those around him who didn't understand the workings of the fire service. One guy was giving an uninformed play-by-play description of what he thought the firefighters were doing, flanked by a guy who insisted they were taking too long and wondering why they didn't already have water flowing on the flames. Mike bit his tongue as he listened to this sideline quarterbacking by those who had never played the game.

He knew that the reason his colleagues didn't run frantically around the scene like people thought they should was because it created disorder and chaos, which resulted in mistakes and accidents. There were plans of attack and clearly delineated roles that everyone had to follow in order to provide the greatest outcome with the fewest injuries.

But it would have been futile to try and explain this to people who were inadvertently making themselves part of the drama unfolding before them.

Mike watched as a group of firefighters donned their air packs, grabbed their tools, and began making their way onto the adjacent rooftops to halt the fire's progress. Torrents of water began streaming onto the blaze from the ground and from aerial ladders while officers directed efforts from every conceivable vantage point.

He knew these men, all of them. He had volunteered for this department early into his training and still stopped by on occasion to catch up with the "old guys" and meet some of the new faces. But from this distance, with the thick smoke billowing everywhere, it was impossible to read the name emblazoned across the back of each turnout coat, let alone recognize faces.

The smell of thick smoke, flames fighting to devour everything in their path, the heat, the constant, seemingly unintelligible sounds from the radios, the chain of command, the teamwork. Mike was never more aware of how much he loved the job, the whole life of the fire service, as he was standing at the edge of a fire scene. Fire was terrifying to watch and intoxicating to battle, making the job one of the greatest rewards in his life. He worked with a group of people who had the same intrinsic desire to be part of something bigger than themselves, he got to help people in their time of need, and he received a paycheck for doing the very thing he couldn't imagine living without. The obvious risks set aside, there was little about this job he didn't admire.

"What was that?" shouted a bystander, pointing at one of the adjacent roofs. "They hit him! They just hit that guy!" All at once everyone seemed to be looking and pointing in the same direction. "There's a firefighter down!" Mike didn't hear the last comments; he was already halfway down the stairwell that led back to the street.

BAPTISM BY FIRE

⁓

Noᴠᴇᴍʙᴇʀ ɪꜱ ᴀ ʙᴇᴀᴜᴛɪꜰᴜʟ month in northern California. The heat of the Indian summer has finally dissipated, taking with it the threat of wild land and brush fires, which are so brutal to fight. With much of Petaluma surrounded by farmland and rolling hills, that type of fire had dominated the summer months that year. It had been one of the busiest seasons of the dozen or so years Jeff Holden had been with the department. He had been filling his off days, and most of his on days, with captain's training, and had received a hard-earned promotion only four and a half weeks earlier.

Things had finally settled down with the fire department schedule, and they were getting back into a routine of taking their four days off without the constant interruption of overtime. It seemed like families had been back from summer vacation with kids back in school for only a couple of months, and already his wife was talking about holiday shopping.

It was a rare opportunity he should probably take advantage of. Cathe, his wife of twelve years, had been working constantly since they moved into their new ranch home. She had been cleaning, hauling things to the dump, hanging drapes, painting, and trying to turn their well-worn find into a cozy home for them and their three children. He had to admit, she was an amazing woman. She drove a hard bargain and could be a formidable force when trying to get a project completed, but she was a lovely and talented wife. Hard to believe this country boy had roped himself a woman who was not only an accomplished interior decorator and graphic artist, but a good wife and mother as well.

The last of his yard work could wait until his next four days off so he and Cathe could take a break, go to lunch, and do some (oh, this was going to be painful) early Christmas shopping. They jumped into Jeff's '65 Ford pickup, which was referred to as the "possum rig," and headed for town.

Cathe had a place in mind for lunch, a cute café on Kentucky Street, followed by a stroll through the antique shops and boutiques to find some of the hidden treasures that always seemed to catch her eye.

The truck bumped and rumbled its way down the back roads into town as Jeff and Cathe discussed all the minutiae of life that were so important to staying connected: how the kids were doing, what had been going on at work, their plans for the holidays.

Cathe was telling Jeff about a new project she was planning when she saw that far-off look in his eyes.

"Jeff?" she inquired.

"That doesn't look good," he said.

"What doesn't look good?"

"Look." He pointed out the windshield to a small, almost indiscernible pillow of black smoke beginning to stretch upward over the part of town they were heading for. "We need to get to Station Two," he said, creating a cloud of dust as he veered off the side of the road to begin a U-turn and head for the station that held his firefighting gear.

Two short turns—and speed and agility the truck hadn't seen in years—brought them onto a main road heading for Station Two. They had gone less than a mile before they saw the ladder truck screaming its way into town.

Jeff ran quickly into the apparatus bay, threw his turnout gear onto Engine Two, and called dispatch. "This is Captain Holden in at Station Two, what have we got?" The dispatcher gave him as much information as they had, and indicated that there were other firefighters on their way in. Marty Farina and Craig Marston arrived within minutes and jumped into their turnout gear, and moments later the three of them were racing lights and sirens into town. Cathe got behind the wheel of the possum rig and headed after them. She had never seen her husband fight a fire before.

She watched in amazement from the second story landing of a bank only a few hundred yards away as Jeff prepared to be baptized as a captain on his first big fire. She kept thinking how odd it was that she'd married Jeff three days before he'd gotten hired as a fireman twelve years ago, and had yet to see him actually do his job. The pride and love she felt for him at this moment were mixed with tendrils of fear as she saw him taking orders and preparing to head for the roof.

He listened carefully to the instructions: station the men on the roof, have them vent the peaks, and stop the fire from devouring the entire strip of historic buildings. There were eight men to supervise on the roof. His job was to ensure that they went to the right spots and did their jobs successfully. He was also to watch over them for unforeseen hazards. He had just left the side of one firefighter who'd been assessing the rooftop through the haze of smoke before trench-cutting, and had climbed over the peak to work with the one of the rookies.

Sean McCarthy was a big kid, six foot one, two hundred and forty-five pounds, and looked far more like Dudley Do-Right than anyone admitted. He worked hard, could be relied on, and was an immediate fit in the department. There was that one time the firemen had taken him aside at a Christmas party and made sure his size, good looks, and new uniform didn't go to his head, but Sean always maintained a modicum of fire department–approved humility. Jeff was grateful he had such a solid group to supervise.

There was a lot to think about as a new captain, and Jeff felt ready for the opportunity. He had fought many a fire not unlike this one and knew instinctively what needed to be done. Barring any unforeseen problems, this fire would be a good first to have under his belt in his new capacity as captain. The only hitch, as he liked to say, was the fact that they were working in a mutual-aid capacity. Engines and firefighters from neighboring towns were arriving to provide support and apparatus, which caused communications to be less than fluid. With the intense level of radio traffic going on, Jeff had to motion to a nearby ladder truck to back away from the portion of roof where his firefighters were working. He hoped the firefighter controlling the ladder's hose could see his signals through the thick veil of smoke.

The roar of water was deafening, making the radios almost impossible to hear. Jeff motioned again for the ladder truck's manhole-sized stream to be moved away from the roof peak. It was too close to the men who were trench-cutting. "Move!" he was yelling in vain to the men who couldn't hear him. Slowly the enormous stream of water began to move to the left, dropping its height at the same time. Jeff looked over in time to see the direction in which the water was going.

His men, oh dear Lord, his men.

SURROUND AND DROWN

~⌒~

IN LARGE FIRE DEPARTMENTS the truck companies and engine crews have two very different roles. The men and women of the truck companies are primarily responsible for the tough hands-on work. They get some glory for their aggressive ventilation and search-and-rescue responsibilities. Inside the circle of firefighting they are referred to simply as "truckees." The engine crews, on the other hand, are responsible for doing most of the hose work—putting the fires out.

In David Halberstam's remarkable book *Firehouse,* he addresses this rivalry by cleverly quoting an engine crew member commenting about truckees getting most of the medals during the New York City Fire Department's annual Medal Day.

"Privately we call it Truck Appreciation Day, we feel they really deserve the medals because we're so busy putting out the fires and having all the real fun, so they ought to get something to compensate." The truckees say that all engine men are terrible cooks, that the engines get lost all the time, and that they couldn't find a fire without the help of a truck. Because of that, they never go anywhere alone. Besides, the truckees note, since the engine men have to get down low to fight a fire, sometimes crawling once they're inside a building to get under the heat, all engine men are short and stubby.

In smaller departments, however, firefighters are commonly cross-trained on both the engine and the ladder trucks, removing much of the stereotypical differences between them. This was the case in Dan's department.

Apart from the situations with engine crew and ladder trucks, there are also delineations in the positions taken on the scene of a fire. A fire where there is a good chance the building will be saved from total loss would require a more offensive attack, salvaging as much of the structure as possible. A defensive position is taken when a building is "fully involved" with the fire. This requires firefighters to use their efforts to protect surrounding areas and structures from being affected by the fire. But there is an exception to these guidelines: when a row of buildings is threatened. In this case firefighters are working to both protect and prevent—to protect existing buildings and to prevent the spread of fire to others.

This is the situation Jeff found himself in at this moment. A ladder truck would not normally be shooting water over a roof where firefighters were offensively trying to protect an adjacent structure. But this fire was requiring a surround-and-drown approach, where the majority of effort was put into getting water on buildings to contain the existing blaze.

Cathe couldn't believe her eyes. One minute she was watching Jeff, easily identified by the red helmet he wore to delineate him from the yellow helmets of the line firefighters, the next she was watching a firefighter being hit by a huge stream of water, blown across the roof like a leaf pushed down a driveway by a high-powered garden hose.

She let out a gasp, gripping the rail before her, and stood transfixed as she watched the firefighter slam into the parapet wall that separated the building they were trying to save from the building that was fully engulfed in flames. She held her breath, tears in her eyes, expecting to see the firefighter disappear over the edge of the building he had been working on only a few moments ago. Time seemed to stand still, and everything began to move in slow motion. Jeff was on the radio, presumably calling for help, and men began to converge upon the injured firefighter. She could see the injured man clutching his chest and assumed by the urgency of the efforts that he was badly injured. Thank God it wasn't Jeff—but whose husband, brother, or son had just been hit? Cathe would not leave the spot until she watched Jeff climb back down off of that roof several hours later.

FIREFIGHTER DOWN

"Nooooo!" was the last thing Jeff remembered yelling before seeing the firefighter hit by the enormous stream of water. He was immediately on the radio indicating, "Firefighter down, we've got a firefighter down on the roof!" His instincts told him to run to the firefighter and do everything he could to help, but his battalion chief was quick to remind him, "Don't get involved in the rescue, you're in charge of the roof, take care of the other men." His desire to get involved was at war with his newfound responsibilities to supervise as a captain. He quickly looked over the western edge of the roof to verify that the Rapid Intervention Crew was being deployed.

The ladder truck operator, immediately notified of the accident created by his master stream, had shut the water down and begun lowering the ladder onto the roof to form a makeshift gangplank that would provide rapid access for the rescue team. Paramedic firefighters swiftly gathered the necessary emergency equipment and made their way to the roof.

They worked gently and efficiently to remove the firefighter's air pack and noted that his helmet had been torn off by the impact. His head was held still as a cervical collar was applied to protect him from neck injuries while an oxygen mask was administered to help with the shortness of breath. The only words they'd heard him speak were, "I can't breathe."

He was expertly placed into a Stokes litter, a basket used to carry him to a waiting ambulance.

Jeff continued to work professionally and efficiently to keep operations uninterrupted as the other men worked feverishly to control the blaze. Not a person on that roof could see the tiniest break in his confidence, but all the while he struggled to suppress the feelings of failure. His first job as a captain and he had failed to protect all of his men. It would be weeks before he would be able to reconcile this feeling.

"CALL MY WIFE"

B<small>Y THE TIME</small> Mike Ortelle reached the fire zone, an area reserved as a command center for fire personnel, the Rapid Intervention Crew was being deployed to the roof. Mike stood unnoticed by officers who worked with experienced resolve to maintain the situation, remove the injured firefighter, and continue to direct efforts to control the blaze that still threatened to spread out of control.

The basket that held the injured firefighter was carefully making its way to the sidewalk below, lowered into the waiting hands of firefighter paramedics who would prepare him for transport to the trauma center.

Mike edged his way toward the head of the basket to

identify the injured fireman. He reeled from the recognition. This was not just one of the firemen he'd come to know on a casual basis during his occasional visits to the firehouse. This was a friend, a man whose children played with his own, a man who sat in his living room drinking coffee, laughing at life, and comparing stories. This was a man whose family sat beside his own on Sunday mornings. He instinctively reached out to grab his friend's hand as the injured fireman looked up into his eyes. The recognition was instantaneous, the words labored and fought for, the message immediate: "Call my wife."

"CODE 3 TO MEMORIAL"

DAN CRINGED WITH PAIN as the gurney came to an abrupt halt in the ambulance and was locked into place. He wanted desperately to free himself from the claustrophobic constraints of the litter he was strapped into to sit up and catch his breath.

"God help me," he thought. "I can't breathe," he mouthed to Jude Prokop, who climbed in as the attending paramedic.

"Get another paramedic," Jude shouted out the back of the ambulance before the doors were closed.

Eli Crombach quickly slid in beside Jude. "I've got your back, Jude, what do you need?"

"Cut his coat off," Jude directed.

"Code 3 to Memorial!" Jude shouted to the firefighter in the driver's seat. "And make it quick!"

Eli went to work cutting off Dan's turnout coat as Jude set up IVs to be started in both arms.

A cardiac monitor was placed on Dan's chest and a pulse-ox device was placed on his finger to monitor oxygen saturation in his blood.

Dan grimaced as he felt every bump and turn the ambulance made as if he were being dragged behind it on a board.

"I'm suffocating," Dan thought to himself. "I'm never going to make the twenty-minute ride to the trauma center."

A CHANGE OF PLANS

ANOTHER DAY'S PLANS thwarted by overtime. So much for the surprise picnic lunch I'd planned in the park; we had to go for what was behind curtain number two. I had been promising my neighbor, Jen, I'd take her up to see my brother Mike's new house at some undisclosed time in the future. The requisite freedom had just been thrust upon me. I had already cleared it with Mike a few days earlier. There was a key under the mat anytime we wanted to come up. Jen had agreed to apply her innate sense of style and interior decorating to Mike's new place, giving him a few ideas to get his home ready in time for the family gathering planned for the Thanksgiving holiday.

It was working out to be a perfect time for us. Dan and I would be celebrating our ten-year wedding anniversary in three days, and I looked forward to spending the holiday with most of my immediate family in another week. Even though Dan was going to be at the firehouse, we'd arranged our schedules so the kids and I would arrive just around dessert time. There was no chance that dessert would be affected by a call, as the wives always prepared those goodies in advance. It was a win/win situation.

"Jen, does Mark know the number where we're going to be?" I queried, for no reason other than that we had left her husband in charge of their three small children without much notice while I whisked her away for a day of decorating. It's pretty common knowledge that most women don't trust their husbands to keep the children alive in their absence, so I knew we should have left Mark with the number in case he needed to know where they kept the milk, food, or diapers.

"No," she surmised after giving it a moment's thought. "We should probably call and give him the number when we get there."

"Roger that," I responded in my attempt to be humorous. She got it.

"I'll call him when we arrive, and quit calling me Roger." We giggled. My kids sat unamused by our conversation in the confines of their car seats, but we knew we were funny mommies.

Jen and I didn't rush right into the house. We let the kids run around the property to expel some energy before we asked them to come in. Temporarily satisfied with their release of energy, the kids settled in before a short video while Jen and I embarked on the beginning of our extreme makeover tour. With my brother and his family gone for the day, we had the place to ourselves. As we stepped into the first room, my nephew's bedroom, the phone began to ring. I stared at the jiggling little NASCAR phone on his nightstand for what seemed an eternity. Why would I answer that? No one knows we're here, my brother has an answering machine, and it's not my house. But something compelled me to pick up the phone and speak into the undercarriage of the car.

"Hello?"

"Sue? It's Mark."

"Hey, Mark, how'd you find us? We were just going to call you with the number."

"It's in your emergency contact book. Listen, Sue, Dan's had an accident at the fire, they're taking him to the trauma center. You need to go there right away."

The trauma center? My emergency contact book? What was Mark doing in my house? What was he talking about? I dropped the phone and ran the few steps to the living room. "Kids, it's an emergency, Daddy's been hurt, everybody into the van!" We whispered desperate prayers and headed for the trauma center.

It was then that I heard God's voice. "Get in the wheel-barrow."

My heart pounded in my throat as Jen and I drove in a blur. "Dear Lord, don't let him die." Memories of long ago chased me back to my past.

I was paralyzed, watching as nurses and doctors worked feverishly to prolong the life of my boyfriend, Brian, injured in a motorcycle accident on the freeway. His head and chest were wrapped in bandages, his eyes bruised and swollen shut. A respiratory tech stood solemnly at the head of the gurney forcing air into his lungs—squeeze, release, pause, squeeze, release, pause. My head pounded with the reality of the inevitable. Brian was not going to live. I stood there in my paramedic uniform, helpless to do anything but watch his life slowly drain away. I stumbled down the hallway to the family waiting area and sobbed into the lap of Brian's mother.

"Oh, please, God, not again." We pulled into the hospital parking lot, the same hospital where Brian lost his life.

I removed Michael from his car seat as Jen took over the wheel, ferrying the older children home to wait for news of their daddy's condition. My heart broke that I couldn't stay and comfort them, but I had to get inside.

The firemen were waiting. Jude, one of the paramedic firefighters who brought Dan to the hospital, put a sympathetic arm around me. "Don't fall apart," I told myself.

"Keep it together." He gently explained the situation. While working on a roof, Dan was struck from behind by a master stream of water from a ladder truck. The fireman directing the water had been momentarily blinded. It was an accident. Of course it was—they do a dangerous job, they are well trained, and there are risks.

Dan had been taken to X-ray. His body was being scanned to determine the extent of his injuries. I was ushered into the family waiting area, where firefighters stood everywhere—some pacing, some talking, all somber, waiting. What are the injuries? How bad are they? Will he live? There are no answers.

The trauma surgeon approached with the preliminary test results. His words sounded unreal. Dan had five broken ribs, two broken vertebrae, a separated shoulder, a bruised heart, and a collapsed lung. Time was imperative. The collapsed lung was compromising his breathing. They would need to cut into his chest and insert a tube to reduce the pressure.

My mind swam with the information, trying to keep its head above water. I nodded in dazed understanding and agreement as they prepared Dan for his procedure.

The emergency waiting area overflowed into the hallway with concerned friends and firefighters, all speaking in hushed tones. Painfully aware that I had no control over this event, I longed nevertheless to bargain with God, the whole while aware that no amount of money, time, or effort would change the outcome of this event.

I wanted somebody to tell me that everything was going to be okay, and I wanted that person to be Dan. I wanted him to remind me that the hospital had an excellent staff of trauma doctors and nurses, convincing me that they would do everything possible to save him. If someone could please tell them he has a wife and five children who love him and need him to come home. It doesn't matter how badly he is broken, just tell me that he will come home.

How I wished I could go back in time and rewrite that moment. The rewrite would include anything but waiting in an emergency room for news of my husband's condition. Dan wouldn't have answered his cell phone that morning and we would be sitting in a park watching Ben and Bailey swing to their hearts' content while the little boys chased a group of irritated ducks around a tree-lined pond.

But Dan wouldn't have rewritten this moment. He wouldn't have had it any other way. He certainly wouldn't have chosen to be hurt—no fireman would—but he certainly wouldn't have passed up the opportunity to fight fire with the group of men he admires most. He memorized and believed in the Fireman's Prayer that hung proudly on the wall of the family room next to a wall unit of firefighter-related memorabilia.

When I am called to duty, God
Wherever flames may rage
Give me strength to save some life
Whatever be its age

Help me embrace a little child
Before it is too late
Or save an older person from
The horror of that fate

Enable me to be alert and
Hear the weakest shout
And quickly and efficiently
To put the fire out

I want to fill my calling and
To give the best in me
To guard my every neighbor
And protect their property

And if according to your will
I have to lose my life
Please bless with your protecting hand
My family, children, and my wife

The initial shock of the accident began to wane as I reflected upon our life together. His career, the one that at times fills me with pride and admiration, had suddenly become a source of uncertainty and sorrow, an intrusion into the life that might have been lived more predictably had he chosen another line of work, one that didn't require him to be in harm's way every time he put on the uniform.

After years on the job, the thought probably doesn't even cross his mind anymore. Each call is incrementally more familiar and routine. But this fact has not kept me from thinking about the choice he makes every day to run into situations that everyone else is running out of.

The feelings of resentment and fear I suppress daily threaten to smother my hope as I think about how things might have been had he chosen a normal career.

We could have lived the life that I imagine is so comfortable for others.

Even if this career has been an adjustment for me, I can reassure myself with the thought that the children do not miss what they have never known. This harried life as a fireman's family is normal to them. They don't see Dan's schedule as inconvenient or invading of our life, they see it for what it is—a reality of the work he does. They are proud of him, proud to be able to say, "My daddy's a fireman." They are not jealous of the time he's gone or the people he works with. They are glad that it gives them an opportunity to visit him when he's gone for extended shifts, loving the time and attention shown them by the firemen he works with every time we're at the firehouse.

They're already in the capable hands of the fire department, as off-duty firefighters ensured that the children were delivered safely home to caring neighbors who had been alerted to the situation after Jen dropped me off. Procedures were being put into place with my family as the focus that I didn't know about. Men were being assigned to ensure that everything was being taken care of in my home as I waited for news of Dan's condition. Dan's battalion chief ordered firemen to stay with me until he could arrive and take over supervision of the situation. The fire that brought Dan here was still being fought by all the available hands from the department and mutual aid from other departments, all the while his department was ensuring I was not left alone.

There was already a steady stream of firefighters from outlying areas arriving at the hospital, some who didn't even know Dan, offering sympathy and support. An invisible network of information was being passed through firefighting channels, bringing encouragement from every direction. The shock of the accident was buffeted by men and women who promised to stay by my side no matter what happened as I became vastly aware that I would not be forced to face this trial alone.

Firefighters dotted the hallways of the emergency waiting area like a band of guardian angels, many of them content to stand quietly, waiting for news of Dan's condition so they could implement the next steps in the process of caring for the children and me. There would be a firefighter assigned to me if I became widowed, to ensure that the children and I would be taken care of for the rest of our lives. His department would do their best to oversee the care of my home and family, to remember my children's birthdays, to meet our needs and fill in the voids left in the wake of a fallen firefighter.

Jude continued to run interference for every issue that came up, ushering me to a private waiting area, ensuring that I had direct access to a phone, screening visitors, and answering questions on my behalf. I was in a cocoon of protection that reduced external pressure and influences, allowing me to focus on the moment's priority.

It was an eerie feeling to be surrounded by men and women enveloping me in their protective circle as if I were suddenly one of them. I could do little but accept everything being done on our behalf, and walk through the moment with this incredible force around me.

WAITING

⁓

"Excuse me, are you the fireman's wife?"

The trauma doctor approached with compassion in his eyes. My heart leaped to my throat as I struggled to swallow, and blue figures drew protectively around me. I rocked nervously under the guise of comforting the baby who slept soundly in my arms, unaware of the chain of events surrounding him.

A chest tube had been inserted between the ribs under Dan's left arm, releasing the air and blood that were accumulating outside his lung. He was breathing on his own with the help of a pump that would keep his lung from collapsing and was being prepared at this moment for transfer to the Intensive Care Unit (ICU). His status was considered critical but stable until the next several hours revealed if there were any hidden injuries.

I was chaperoned to the third floor and into the ICU waiting room, where family members were kept apart from critically ill or injured loved ones by a set of metal security doors. Hours had somehow slipped by, during which time Dan's parents had arrived. They encouraged me to return home to try and get a few hours of sleep and check on the children. But I was unable to muster the courage to leave, feeling that somehow my very presence ensured that nothing more could go wrong.

Finally, several hours later and consumed by fatigue, I gave in to the need for rest and was given a ride home. Our neighbor Deb was waiting for my arrival with a cup of tea at the ready and an immediate hand with the baby. With Michael tucked comfortably into his crib, I quickly glanced in on the other children and tried to kiss their heads without disturbing them. Ben was the first to sit up from his position on the top bunk. "Mom, how's Dad?" I explained things the best I could while trying to reassure him that Daddy was in the best possible place to get better. Matthew began stirring in the bottom bed as I tried to quietly finish reassuring Ben.

"Mommy?" questioned the miniature version of Dan under Ben's bunk. "I don't want to be a fireman anymore."

The statement preceded an onslaught of tears. Both boys were suddenly in my lap as I whispered words of hope and encouragement, much like the hope and encouragement I had been receiving only hours before.

My restless sons followed me into our room and positioned themselves securely on Daddy's side of the bed. I slipped in, exhausted, beside them, for the few hours of sleep I would get before returning to the hospital.

"Sue? Hi, it's Bobbie, I wanted to catch you before you left for the hospital again," said Brian's mother. She knew better than anyone what memories this event would stir up for me. We had maintained our contact and friendship since Brian's death years earlier. "I saw the article in the paper today, have you seen it?"

No, I replied, I had not seen the paper.

"Don't look at it if you can avoid it," was the warning. "You don't need to see the photo at this point." I thanked her for her support, put the paper out of my mind, got dressed, got the baby up, and headed for the hospital.

The ICU waiting room was not what I expected, considering I was arriving at the crack of dawn. Crisp blue uniforms lined the halls just outside the waiting area, with many of the men and women sitting respectfully in the room anticipating the family's arrival. Again, firefighters, some of whom I had never seen or met, offered their unconditional support at this difficult time. I was overcome with emotion at this outpouring of kindness and support. But I stopped short at a picture lying benignly on the table before me. The front page of the local paper showed Dan, lying on the roof, clutching his chest, his gentle face a mixture of anguish and pain. The newspaper photographer had gotten a rare photo op when he captured this shot from an adjacent building, never anticipating that the fireman he had focused on would suddenly be struck and injured. The picture was truly worth a thousand words, some of which I dared not utter at this moment. My appreciation for the power of that photo would come at a later date, once I knew for sure that it wouldn't be the last picture I would ever see of him.

I waited as the fireman in charge for the day, keenly sensitive to my plight, reported to the staff that I had arrived and requested that I be allowed to see Dan.

"Mrs. Farren, you can come in for just a minute," indicated a nurse in muted scrubs, motioning for me to follow her through the intimidating metal security doors. I slipped my newborn son into the waiting arms of Dan's mother and followed my escort into her world.

I walked softly into the room, my footsteps hesitant. The machines blinked and whirred, displaying numbers and rates for the discerning eyes of the nurses and doctors. Dan was still. Flecks of sawdust and smudges of soot still lingered on his face and neck, a reminder of what brought him here. Tubes and wires attached to his body snaked through blankets and bedrails, each one with a purpose.

"*Phhhhht . . . whoosh . . . phhhhhht . . . whoosh . . .*" The pump kept his lung from collapsing. Turning his head slowly, his eyes flickered, then opened. A small smile formed at the corner of his mouth as I came into view.

"I'm okay . . . we'll be okay," he whispered with a hoarse voice. I leaned cautiously over the rail, careful to avoid the maze of tubes, and kissed the face of the man I loved, the man God had spared.

"Go home and get some sleep, I'll still be here tomorrow," he admonished gently, not knowing a night had already passed. Not even his injuries could keep him from looking out for me. Always the fireman.

I don't care if our life is not "normal," my calendar a mess, our holidays and family celebrations unpredictable. It doesn't matter that this career and life require difficult choices and competing emotions. I am not troubled by the uncertainty of life at this moment.

I am grateful, because my husband is going to live.

THE FIREMAN'S WIFE

"Excuse me, are you the fireman's wife?" As I prepared to answer that question for the third time in twenty-four hours, I was hit with the revelation of all the things that had brought me to this moment. Each step appeared to be a piece of a puzzle that was coming together before my eyes to reveal an intricate path—a path I would not have chosen for myself.

There was a manuscript to complete. A journal of events that had begun only a few months earlier with a title penciled at the top of the page. A journal that would begin with our first days together in this industry and would chronicle the struggles and accomplishments we have had along the way. A journal that would include our most recent experience, an experience that many have been through before and many more fear will come, never able to know the outcome, an experience that would give me the confidence to tell my story.

I recalled the sensation of doom that had flooded over me in the weeks prior to Dan's accident, reminding me to pray for him morning and night. It might have been nerves or hormones, but it appeared to have been more of a message at this point.

The overwhelming desire to focus my nesting instincts on something other than cleaning, a desire that led me to make that emergency contact book out of an unused notebook that sat beneath the phone in my family room. The book that my neighbor's husband, Mark, was able to find, leading him to the number of my brother's home.

Our good friend Mike Ortelle, seeing the column of smoke and going to be of help. Entering the fire zone and going to the litter being lowered from the roof, shocked to find himself looking into the eyes of his friend, Mike would call his wife, Liz, who would try in vain to reach me at home and then have the foresight to call our neighbor, whom they also knew from church, and tell him to break into my house if he had to and find the number where I was. She was sure that I would have the numbers written somewhere.

The photographer who had positioned himself across the street to chronicle the fire events, who instead got a graphic picture of my husband's first moments after the accident. The picture that would lead to a follow-up article on our family, our faith, and my husband's gratefulness to be alive.

I can still hear the race car phone jingling in my mind as I stared at it and wondered why I had such a compelling desire to answer a call that couldn't possibly be for me, the call leading me back to the trauma center that had held such sorrow for me in the past. The painful memory would be softened by a different outcome this time.

I would come face to face with my fears as the firemen waited anxiously for my arrival at the hospital. They placed their support and comfort around me to ensure that I did not face this trial alone, these men who would risk their own lives to save my husband's.

I will go through whatever my husband's accident requires of us. I will write the book that has planted itself in the corners of my mind. I will walk this path with the faith that has brought me to this point. I will gladly toast my ten-year wedding anniversary sitting on the edge of a hospital bed with a paper cup full of sparkling cider and a bowl of red Jell-O.

"Yes, I am the fireman's wife."

GOING HOME

SOMEHOW WE HAD SURVIVED those first few days in the ICU regardless of my husband's efforts. He had been gently reprimanded and relegated to bed until the doctors and nurses deemed him strong enough to stand without falling. He would be transferred out of the ICU after the bleeding in his chest had stopped and he was strong enough to blow into a device that indicated he was breathing sufficiently, a device that he kept next to him in bed and practiced blowing into every three minutes for the next three days until he had won his coveted release ticket to the rehab ward on the fourth floor.

The only question that took second place to "When can I go home?" was the ever-popular "When can I go back to work?" The doctors were a little more evasive with those answers, trying instead to keep him focused on his recovery. But the hope of returning to work was in fact pivotal to his recovery. Everything for him would be focused around that goal. The doctors were careful not to tell him that there was a chance he would never return to his line of work again, his injuries potentially affecting his upper body so dramatically that he might not ever be capable of doing the job he loved. It was news that only I had been given, and I knew to keep it to myself.

I watched patiently as Dan stood to cautiously remove his hospital gown, which the other firemen and I liked to refer to as his "nightie." Setting the gown on the bed's edge, Dan cautiously took the denim shirt I held for him and awkwardly slid his right arm into the first sleeve, finally resigning himself to ask for help with the left, still painful and numb in places where nerves were cut when placing his chest tube. I had waited for Dan to ask for my help and didn't coddle him the way I'd wanted to. I knew that his recovery was going to be a learning experience for both of us.

The local paper whisked in for a quick interview and photo of the recovering firefighter for the next day's paper. The quickly expanding but still close-knit community was eager for news of the injured fireman's progress.

The photo and interview completed, a nurse entered the room with a wheelchair and informed my husband that he wouldn't be leaving the hospital unless he agreed to sit in the hospital-provided chariot. He relented with a shy smile, knowing his pride would not win this battle.

We descended gently to the first-floor lobby. The bright colors, potted plants, and fresh air were a welcome change from the sterility of the hospital room. The glass doors before us slid effortlessly apart, ushering us into the sun-dappled parking lot where the last leg of the journey home would begin.

Dan squeezed my hand as he fought to not give way to the emotion he felt at the scene before us. Sunshine danced off the recently shined chrome of fire engines and ambulances as a parade of well-wishers, many in uniform, broke into applause at my husband's release. Chris Albertson, a towering and imposing figure with a mane of gray hair and a perpetual scowl, stood humbly at the back of the crowd, alternately applauding and swiping tears from his experienced face. Today was more than a celebration of my husband's survival—it was also Chris's one-year anniversary as Dan's fire chief. I could only imagine his relief at attending a discharge from the hospital versus what could have easily been a more solemn assembly.

This homegoing would be only one of the many steps in his journey to rehabilitation. The real work was about to begin without limelight or fanfare. We would have to cling to the love and support of these moments to see us through the storms the future was holding for us. Another journey was just beginning as Dan waited impatiently for his body to begin the slow process of healing.

CUT FROM THE CLOTH

THE CHILDREN WAITED anxiously on the front steps of our home for the first glimpse of our minivan bringing Daddy back. Our dear friend Danielle had spent the entire morning with the children helping them to create an enormous butcher-paper poster, each letter, cherishingly imperfect, combined to make the sign that hung on the garage door: WELCOME HOME, DADDY. WE MISSED YOU!!!

Gone was the fireman who waited eagerly for each child to clamber into his arms, as the fragile, broken body of a daddy who could not be hugged or climbed on was helped out of the van. Nine days after his accident he was lucky to be alive, let alone coming home.

The children rushed to his side and gingerly hugged his legs, leading him carefully toward the front door. The doctors had described the impact of the water stream as a pedestrian being hit by a full-speed truck. His entire left side had been shattered, and it would be months before he would be able to embrace the children the way he wanted.

Firemen had been converging on the house for days, trimming trees, mowing lawns, stacking wood, and making our home winter-ready in anticipation of our needs. The house was awash with flowers, cards, and letters, the freezers stuffed with homemade meals from the firemen and their wives. They'd even rearranged the furniture to make access to everything easier for Dan, including the delivery of one of the department recliners, so he could stretch out and sleep without having to be in bed all day. It was also the firemen's way of keeping him from being too homesick for the day room at work.

The recovery process was going to be slow. Days of pain and exhaustion were going to be complicated with setbacks in healing. Days of helping him dress and tie his shoes quickly turned to weeks, with Dan feeling very little improvement in his condition. Physical therapy began immediately to help him get use of his left arm again, still almost immovable from the pain of the shoulder separation and the nerve damage in his chest. There was an addiction issue we were warned about that would come later when they'd eventually wean him off his pain medicine, which he was taking up to six times a day to minimize swelling and reduce the unavoidable discomfort.

Weeks turned to months and the firefighters continued to visit faithfully, doing everything in their power to keep Dan's spirits up and help him to stay motivated to try to return to work. It wasn't that they wouldn't understand if he couldn't make it back, but they were intimately aware of how depressed and discouraged he could become if the end of his career in the fire service was forced upon him before he was ready.

Dan's battalion chief, Mike Ahlin, did everything he could to try and prepare me for the struggles he knew we would face throughout Dan's recovery.

The transition out of the fire service, he warned me, can be very traumatic for career firefighters. Whether it's by injury, illness, or retirement, the loss is akin to losing a dearly loved family member or even separating conjoined twins. The prematurely separated firefighters often experience bouts of depression, mourning the loss of camaraderie and companionship they unconsciously hold to like a lifeline. New careers and hobbies will always be laced with stories of what they used to do. Even if they're off the job, they will always consider themselves firemen for life. The career change I'd always secretly longed for I would never want for him under these conditions.

In the blink of an eye our lives had taken a direction we'd never expected. I had been getting up every morning at 5:00 A.M. while the house was still quiet and spending some time working on writing the story of Dan's career. If I could finish it, Dan would always have the story of this part of his life in writing and would never forget all we'd been through.

As time wore on, I began considering the fact that I might need to go get a job. It became more and more apparent that Dan wasn't getting his strength back. Recent X-rays revealed that the two broken vertebrae in his back were not healing as expected, and the nerve damage in his chest made even the pressure of bedsheets intolerable. With no tangible end in sight, I began considering ways to supplement our income.

Dan's injury pay, which was his base pay without taxes taken out, would be enough to hold us over temporarily, but it was not the same as that of a fireman who worked an overtime shift every tour to make ends meet. We had modified our lifestyle significantly when Dan became a fireman, deciding together that it would be best for me to stay home to raise the children. Shopping sprees at Nordstrom's had given way to bargain hunts at Wal-Mart, and we had walked away from much of what we valued when we had two full-time incomes. We drove cars until they wore out and not until we were bored with them, and the simplicity of living modestly had become the greatest freedom we had ever known. But we were not going to survive on an injured fireman's income. Our savings were slowly being depleted.

I was afraid as we passed the six-month mark—and then the eight-month mark—without improvement, and felt it was time for us to have a talk about our future.

Dan listened patiently, unconsciously cradling his left arm, as I shared my concerns with him. I reassured him that I had no problem with going back to work and that we could find a good school for the children. He could stay home and focus on his rehabilitation until he was strong enough to consider another line of work. I made suggestions for things he could consider doing in the future with the different talents he possessed. He was an intelligent, hard-working man with a strong work ethic and an eye for excellence. Anybody would be lucky to employ him, even if he wasn't able to do physical work. He would be an asset in other ways.

He nodded at all the right times and even appeared to be considering what I was saying, but he was having none of it. He already had a plan of his own, and it didn't include changing careers. He knew before I said a word that this accident would have jarred my insecurities about his career again. But he'd already talked to the chief and wanted to start going back to the fire department in more of an administrative capacity. He didn't care if he had to write reports, do business inspections, or review paper-work, he wanted to get his feet wet again. His rationale was that being back in the atmosphere of the department would be good for his ailing spirits and would keep him motivated to work toward getting strong enough to return to the line.

I balked and protested as much as I thought would be tolerated, to no avail. I didn't want Dan going back into the firehouse yet; it would only discourage him more when he realized he wasn't capable of doing the job. Besides, I was really hoping he would see this as an opportunity to get out of a career that almost cost him his life, a wakeup call of sorts. He knew what had gone unsaid. I didn't want Dan going back to the fire department in any capacity.

I'd done my part, worried, waited, watched, and prayed as he went off each shift to his unpredictable job. We'd accumulated all the fire department–related home dé-cor and clothing I could tolerate. I'd survived the disrupting phone calls, the bumps in the middle of the night, and the well-intentioned questions about my concerns for his safety.

I appreciated all that had been done for us, the love and support, the incredible sense of being a part of something so loyal and honorable. But we had five children to think about, and having a memory instead of a father was not a part of my plan. It was time to move on.

Dan understood my concerns. It wasn't the first time

we'd had this conversation, it had just been many years since it had taken place. He let me wrestle with my feelings, vent them, and put them all out on the table for any rational person to see. He agreed, we had had a close call. The job was at times burdensome and unpredictable. But he waited, much like I do with a child who protests a nap, for me to exhaust myself with my concerns and then took a gentle but firm stand for all that he was fighting for. This career was who he was; it was a part of why he was a good husband and father. I had married him, but I did not own him. He loved me, and would do anything for me, but he would not walk away from his career because I was afraid. There might come a day when he would be incapable of returning, but for now he would continue to fight for his goal.

Three weeks later he gave me two days' notice. Any more would have given me too much time to formulate an elaborate argument. Effective Monday, he would be back in uniform walking the streets doing business inspections. It would require only that he talk to business owners and check emergency exits and fire extinguishers to make sure they were up to code for their own protection and the safety of their patrons. He would not be required to do any manual labor or risk his life. Besides, he justified, it would be an asset to the shift captains who struggled constantly to keep up on the responsibilities of paperwork and inspections while running emergency calls every day.

Guilt. It worked every time.

I conceded to the idea because, as Dan had so clearly indicated, it would truly be a benefit to all involved. Considering the fact that Dan still couldn't pick baby Michael up without grimacing said more about his physical progress than any of the arguments I could offer. I figured the constant walking and movement he would get while doing inspections without the benefit of naps and pain medication would say more than I ever could, and he would reconsider my rationale.

The days were hard. The first few times he returned home after a full day of inspections he went right to bed for a nap. If his days weren't full with work, he would cut out early and go to physical therapy for a couple of hours.

He came in one day from a half-day of business inspections and an afternoon of physical therapy with a broad grin on his face. Nine months of physical therapy and two weeks into his new inspection work, he was delighted to tell me he was no longer doing what he referred to as "girlie" push-ups. He had gone from doing his first few push-ups on the edge of a table to push-ups on the floor using his knees, to regular I-couldn't-do-one-to-save-my-life push-ups.

You'd have thought he'd just been promoted to fire chief for all the emotion this event brought with it. This single accomplishment was all he needed to prove to himself that he would be able to get his strength back. He was convinced he would be given a release back to full duty if he could just "work through the pain," as he would say, and keep pushing himself.

Push-ups at physical therapy became push-ups on my kitchen floor three times a day. He began weaning himself from the medications and was now taking them only at night. I was happy for him: happy that he was getting his strength back, happy to see him picking up the kids (even if he still winced at times), and happy to see him forcing himself off the pain medication, which had taken on a life of its own. I'd seen how dependent he'd become on the temporary relief it afforded him at the end of each day.

Of all the things he struggled with in this time, the addiction had been by far one of the most difficult things to let go of. His ability to fight this dependency was a true test of his determination to return to the job that he'd felt destined for from his earliest days on a Big Wheel.

There were doctors to see and releases to obtain as he worked toward his chance to return to the work of a real firefighter. Much like in the beginning of his career, he would need to prove himself with strength tests. But there was one thing he would have no control over: X-rays.

I took the call from the radiologist and quickly passed

the phone to Dan. The expression on his face said it all. The X-rays had revealed the one thing he had not dared anticipate: the broken parts of his vertebrae—floating breaks, they had called them—had somehow fused together. He was ready to return.

NEVER GIVE UP

⁓

Days filled with pain, frustration, insomnia, tears, depression, and addiction are finally behind us, and I am not ready. Not ready to face the worry, the doubt, and the long hours apart after having a taste of life without the intrusions of worry and overtime.

I'm ready to resort to begging him to change careers, to take the retirement his attorney has encouraged him to take, to cash it all in and drive off into the sunset in our motor home. We could sell the house, he could work at Wal-Mart, and we would be content just being together as a family. He could take any job he wanted that didn't involve flames, things exploding, blood, or anything that included jeopardizing his life. Whatever it was, I would promise not to complain. Florist, car salesman, plumber, tolltaker, he can have it all if he would only hang up the uniform, shove the steel-toed boots to the back of the closet, and put his badge in a glass-covered box. I would make a photo album of his glory days and we could sit in the relative safety and comfort of our home, reminiscing, looking at pictures, grateful that he doesn't fight fire for a living anymore.

He could even visit the firehouse and just hang out with the guys, swapping stories of the "big ones" they've been involved in. He would always be able to pull the ace from his sleeve and tell them of the day he almost lost his life. Laughing with the guys as they compared scars, with a shake of his head he'd say, "Boy, I'm glad I got out when I did. Been there, done that, have the photo album to prove it." Giving them each a friendly clap on the shoulder, he would pass around smiley-face stickers from his new job at Wal-Mart, encouraging them to stop by and see him some time. He'd be sure to get them their public safety discount and maybe a free donut.

But I'm not kidding anybody. The aroma of morning coffee and floor wax would take hold the minute he turned to leave. Walking through the apparatus bay one last time, he would be overcome with fireman's pride as he gazed at the gleaming engines and equipment waiting for the next call to service. His heart would pound with longing as the garage doors groaned to life, familiar dispatch tones beginning: *Structure fire district 1-3 . . . Reported structure fire, smoke and flames showing at 198 D St. Map page "I" Ida 10. Engines 9381 and 9383, Truck 9351 and 9301, and Medic 91 and 93.*

And then he'd know, without a shadow of a doubt, that the firehouse is where he belongs. He is a fireman. No one else in the world understands these feelings like those on the job.

Asking him to give up the fireman's life would be asking him to give up on life itself.

Dan would remind you, as most firefighters would, that he isn't a hero. He's just another person who was fortunate enough to follow his calling. For as long as he is able, he will continue to carry on the imperfect traditions and legacies of the fire service, knowing full well he may one day be called to lay down his life for a stranger.

On September 21, 2003, my husband returned to his first day of active duty since his accident. Twenty-four hours later, as his shift was winding to an end, he was notified that he would need to stay for mandatory overtime. This would be followed by another twenty-four-hour shift and a follow-up officer's class, leaving him gone his first time back for more than eighty hours.

I am tired. The kids are all sick, as is par for the course. And once again, Daddy is at the firehouse.

It has not been easy being a fireman's wife. The life of uncertainty can take its toll. But then I remember my husband is happy, happy to be back on the job, wearing the uniform and going the distance for anyone who needs him. And I am accepting the transition back into the life that I have grown to know and, in spite of its difficulties, love. I am sometimes discouraged and exhausted, sometimes relieved and grateful.

Because for better or worse, in sickness and health, for richer or poorer, in overtime and in inconvenience, I am thankful that God has given me a fireman and proud to say I am a fireman's wife.

GLOSSARY OF TERMS

Apparatus—Firefighting vehicles, engines, trucks, etc.

Battalion chief—Second in command, supervises fire scene.

Captain—Third in command, supervises truck or engine company.

Chief—The big cheese, supervises everybody and everything.

Code 2—An emergency vehicle responding to a call without lights and sirens.

Code 3—An emergency vehicle responding to a call with lights and sirens (means there is a threat of loss of life, limb, or property).

Defensive firefight—Protecting uninvolved buildings from fire.

EMT (Emergency Medical Technician)—A person trained in basic life support.

Engineer—The person who gets to drive the really cool fire engine.

Fire engine—Generally contains three to four firefighters who are responsible for putting the wet stuff on the red stuff.

Firefighters—The people seen running into situations everyone else is running out of.

Fully involved fire—What every firefighter lives for.

Hook and ladder—Fire truck with three to four firefighters who are responsible for breaking down doors, breaking out windows, and cutting large holes in roofs.

Intern—Student, explorer, hopeful.

Litter—A basket used for removing patients from precarious situations.

Master stream—An enormous water stream typically flowing from an aerial ladder or deck gun. Please don't mention it around my husband.

Off line—Temporarily disabled firefighter.

On line—Actively working firefighter.

On-the-job—Currently employed firefighter or police officer.

Paramedic—Individual trained in advanced life support, gets to do all the cool medical stuff like starting IVs, defibrillating patients, giving medications, etc.

Probation—A period of time averaging between twelve and eighteen months for the firefighters to prove they are capable of cooking, cleaning, answering phones, studying, and occasionally fighting fires.

Probie (aka Rookie, Pleeb, New Guy, Boot, Newbie, Hey You)—A term of endearment given to probationary firefighters.

Pulse ox—Device used to measure levels of oxygen in a patient's bloodstream.

Rapid Intervention Crew (RIC)—Firefighting team trained in the immediate rescue of downed firefighters.

Rolling dice (Liar's dice)—A game played after meals that is used to determine who will be washing dishes (assuming there's no probie on duty).

Spouse—The person responsible for handling troubles at home while the firefighter handles everyone else's troubles.

Stokes basket—*See* Litter.

Strike team—A group of firefighters traveling outside their normal jurisdiction to provide extra manpower and resources on really big emergencies.

Trench cut—A hole cut in a roof to release heat and smoke and interrupt the spread of fire.

Truckee—Firefighters who are assigned to work on ladder trucks. They typically consider themselves the real firefighters.

This is by no means an exhaustive list of officers, terms, or definitions, as fire departments and personnel vary.

ACKNOWLEDGMENTS

DURING THE WRITING of this book, it has become apparent how much my life has been touched by the teamwork and way of life that, in the words of Ken Dick, my husband's partner and friend, "is just the fireman's way." This book is in no small part a result of these characteristics. I could write an entire chapter (although I'll try not to) thanking all the firefighters and their families who so graciously took the time to share their stories, experiences, and struggles with me.

First and foremost, I would like to thank the men and women of the Petaluma Fire Department who have taken us into their fold and blessed us with the foundation to paint a picture of our unique fire department family, quirks and all. A special thanks to the wives who took time out of their busy schedules to allow me to interview them and ensure that I was not alone with my issues. I am especially indebted to Nancy Fanucchi, Kathy Lord, Alice Gloeckner, Amy Gloeckner, Polly Hayes, Gloria Epperson, Dee Ahlin, Cathe Holden, Lisa Colorado, Karen Rasmussen, Lisa Schweizer, and Marilyn Albertson for their special contributions, sometimes made without even knowing it.

It is with heartfelt gratitude that I also thank the following people:

To Marsha Marks, who saw the potential of this story before any of us knew we had a book, your passion as an author and support as a friend have been irreplaceable. To Francine Rivers, who believed in me before I believed in myself, you are the epitome of salt and light in your writing and in your life. To my dear friend Christine Jacobs, who provided me with the support and location I needed to complete this project and who knows the true meaning of being an unconditional friend. To my friends Shannon King and Barbara Upham for contributing their time, attention, and talents. To John Fagan, my favorite paramedic dinosaur, who planted the seed for the book to begin. A very special thanks to June Irwin, whose vision and enthusiasm touches the lives of everyone she meets.

Many thanks to our families, for without their support this book would not have been possible. To my sisters, Cindy and Beth, my brother, Mike, and a special thanks to my niece, Dominique, for her friendship and encouragement. Keep writing Nique! To Gerry and Janet Farren, Carol and Allen Covarrubias, and Eileen and Lisa for being such an instrumental part of who Dan is today. Thank you, Lisa, for being my rear guard.

Thank you also to Chris and Marilyn Albertson, for your tireless support and encouragement—we are honored to be a part of your lives. To Kari and Tyler Miller, our answer to prayer, for the love and support you provided to our entire family, especially our children, during this incredibly challenging time—you are the best, Kari! To the other Miller family, with many thanks to Betty, Joanna, Sarah, Mary Frances, and Rebecca for their willingness to review, suggest, and babysit on a moment's notice (and to David, John Andrew, Benjamin, Michael, Elizabeth, Anna Rose, and Abigail for parting with them), may the Lord continue to bless you. Thank you also to Francine Grevin and Scott Roberts—your friendship was the lifeline I needed in my most troubling times, twenty years of friendship unimpeded by life! To Joe and Bobbie McCarthy, who allowed me to share our memories. Thanks as well to Deb Ross, Jen and Mark P., and the entire Ortelle family, for being with us in our crucial moments and beyond; Dr. Anand

Chaudhry and his sidekick Tammy, for making it physically possible for me to complete this project. A special thank you to Karen Salee, who went from being a complete stranger to a dear friend when our children found each other on an otherwise empty beach. It has been an honor to get to know you and a privilege to see the way God uses your incredible talent as an artist. I hope our future includes many more projects together.

Thanks to Battalion Chief Mike Ahlin for ensuring we were well cared for and anticipating our every need; Captain Jeff Holden for setting the standard as a talented, compassionate, and excellent officer; Captain George Vedder for being the self-appointed but greatly appreciated "purveyor of useless knowledge"; and Battalion Chief Mike Haberski for his unorthodox and painfully insightful sense of humor. To Battalion Chief Art Fannuchi, your incredible contribution to the EMS division will be sorely missed. To the nurses and doctors of Santa Rosa Memorial Hospital for your excellent care and commitment to trauma patients. To Dr. Richard Bradley, Houston Fire Department; Battalion Chief Gary Galasso, San Jose Fire Department; Deputy Chief Sheldon Gilbert, Alameda County Fire Department. A special thanks to the Santa Rosa firefighters for introducing me to their wives and loved ones, who let me participate in one of their girls' nights out. Honorable mention goes to the firefighters of the Colorado Springs Fire Department, who welcomed the unknown wife of a fellow firefighter to interrupt the sanctity of a Denver Broncos football game for an interview. You are living proof that the firefighting family knows no boundaries.

It is with deepest gratitude that I thank Will Schwalbe of Hyperion, who took a chance on an unknown housewife with a story to tell. I am eternally grateful for the opportunity I was afforded and the chance to work with the magnificent editor Kelly Notaras, who refined my words without taking away my voice. Thanks also to Danielle Egan-Miller of Browne Miller Literary Agency for representing me on a hunch and a recommendation.

AUTHOR'S NOTE

THROUGHOUT THIS BOOK I have shared in as delicate a way possible the faith that is the very fiber of our family. It is not a particular religion that we subscribe to, but a personal daily walk with God. This relationship is what sustained us through Dan's accident, and it is what keeps me going despite the uncertainty of his career choice.

I am convinced that God does not give us more than we can handle, and we are never alone.

It is with heartfelt sympathy that I remember all the widows, mothers and fathers, friends, and families of those who have given their lives in the line of duty. This sacrifice is summed up best in John 15:13:

"Greater love has no one than this, that he lay down his life for a friend."